*Windows
into the
Past*

CRITICAL PROBLEMS IN HISTORY

*The University of Notre Dame Press gratefully
acknowledges the generous support of alumnus Robert Dilenschneider,
his wife, Jan, and their sons, Geoffrey and Peter,
in the publication of titles in this series.*

Judith M. Brown

Windows
into the
Past

Life Histories and the
Historian of South Asia

University of Notre Dame Press
Notre Dame, Indiana

Library of Congress Cataloging-in-Publication Data

Brown, Judith M. (Judith Margaret), 1944–
    Windows into the past : life histories and the historian of South Asia /
Judith M. Brown.
        p.   cm. — (Critical problems in history)
    Includes bibliographical references and index.
    ISBN-13: 978-0-268-02217-4 (pbk. : alk. paper)
    ISBN-10: 0-268-02217-8 (pbk. : alk. paper)
    1. South Asia—Historiography.   2. India—Historiography.   3. South
Asia—Biography.   4. India—Biography.   5. Balliol College (University of
Oxford)—Alumni and alumnae—Biography.   6. Family life—South Asia—
Historiography.   7. Family life—India—Historiography.   8. Gandhi,
Mahatma, 1869–1948.   9. Nehru, Jawaharlal, 1889–1964.   I. Title.
    DS435.B76   2009
    954.0072—dc22

                                                          2009027703

The study of history offers us an opportunity to illuminate the work of institutions and communities, but it often overlooks the lives that are molded by those same social forces. Judith M. Brown, Beit Professor of Commonwealth History and Professorial Fellow of Balliol College, the University of Oxford, is a leading historian of South Asia who has developed a stimulating and provocative technique to conduct historical research. Dr. Brown explores "life histories" of families and institutions, examining them in all their richness while letting readers peer into captivating "windows into the past."

In her scholarly work Professor Brown observes, "there is much to be gained from moving beyond the study of groups of similar people to a longitudinal study of families and the study of the life of different sorts of critical institutions." Her astute exploration of family life history reveals patterns over the course of generations that ultimately provide telling insights into people and communities who often left little historical documentation that could assist researchers.

In recent decades the study of history itself has become a contentious issue. How we interpret the past, often through the lens of politics, religion, and ideology, says a great deal about a society. It affects the present and can direct or misdirect the future. As the author says, "The practice of history is also consistently on the move, as contemporary issues suggest new interpretations of the past or new problems to examine, and as development in neighboring disciplines suggest new intellectual and scholarly problems and routes into the study of the past."

The Dilenschneider family is very proud to support this remarkable historical project, the second in the "Critical Problems in History" series published by the University of Notre Dame Press. It is preceded in this series by Doris L. Bergen's *The Sword of the Lord: Military Chaplains from the First to the Twenty-First Century*. These works are truly a credit to Notre Dame and the scholars who produced them.

—Robert L. Dilenschneider

Contents

Illustrations

Acknowledgments

This volume began life with the invitation from the History Department at the University of Notre Dame, to give a series of lectures in April 2008 on an aspect of the practice of history, generously endowed by an alumnus of the university, Robert Dilenschneider. I would like to thank him for making my visit possible, and also for his commitment to the historian's craft as an interesting and important one. It is a commitment I share; and, as I indicate in my introduction, I also believe that professional historians should communicate not only with their colleagues and students, but with a wider public who show a hunger for different types of history. I wish to thank two successive heads of the History Department who extended such a warm welcome to me, Professors James Turner and John T. McGreevy. The former suggested that I might speak about the historian as biographer, and it was my rather strong reaction to this suggestion that opened up the idea of varieties of life history as the topic for my lectures. To their colleagues I would also give my thanks for the enormously enjoyable week my husband and I spent in their company, and that of their students, while I was giving the lectures. The production of this volume would not have been possible without the skills of the staff of the University of Notre Dame Press, and I thank Barbara Hanrahan particularly for working with me on this.

I should also note with gratitude the people who and institutions that gave permission for the use of the illustrations: they are noted in the list of illustrations. Ms. Anna Sander, Lonsdale Curator at Balliol College, shared with me her skills and enthusiasm for archives in preparing these for publication. Dr. John Jones, Archivist and Emeritus Fellow of Balliol College, gave me much help in understanding the history of the college, in matters both serious and more frivolous. My two students whose personal names appear in chapter 3 I would like to thank while preserving their anonymity, as also my colleague at London University who generously shared her husband's family's migratory history with me.

Introduction

The Practice of History

This book is based on a series of lectures on the practice of history given in the History Department at the University of Notre Dame in 2008. As a practitioner of imperial and global history, and, in particular, of the history of South Asia and South Asians outside that subcontinent, I found this invitation exciting and challenging. History is perhaps more than almost any other discipline a contentious business, and inevitably political, because it deals with the past of women and men in society, and so has profound consequences for how people as individuals and groups interpret their pasts and presents, and draw on their pasts to try to fashion their futures. It is hardly surprising that the leaders of modern nation-states have paid such attention to how history is taught in schools, or that politicians and ideologues use different understandings of the past as they interpret and invent the present. In the case of South Asia, for example, the partition of old imperial India in 1947 is a deeply emotive historical event, playing a crucial but very different part in the national histories of India and Pakistan, as each state has sought to explain its political origins and ideological orientation. Or as another example, in India specifically, history has become a deeply contentious aspect of recent imaginings of India as a Hindu rather than a plural or composite nation. The practice of history is also consistently on the move, as contemporary issues suggest new interpretations of the past or new problems to examine, and as developments in neighbouring disciplines suggest new intellectual and scholarly problems and routes into the study of the past.[1]

South Asian history as now practised is a comparatively modern field, originating in the 1960s in the aftermath of the end of empire, at a time when new sources were becoming rapidly available for the academic study of the history of the subcontinent. It has become an intensely vibrant and contested branch of the wider discipline of history. At first South Asian history was dominated by the themes of state and nation, as scholars sought from different perspectives to understand the nature of the imperial state with its institutional structures and underlying alliance structures in Indian society, and its evidently growing weaknesses in the years before 1947. Interwoven with this was an examination of the emerging and often conflicting senses of nationalism on the subcontinent and the nature of the political movements that claimed to speak in the name of the nation. Towards the end of the twentieth century this essentially political focus had shifted, under the influence of several wider trends in the practice of history. Prominent among these influences were the emergence of women's history, which led historians of India to see the pervasive role of gender, understood more broadly than women's experience, in the history of imperialism and of nationalism; recognition of the importance of ecological history; and the flowering of what in European contexts was called "history from below" or the study of poorer and less powerful people who had so often been left out of the historical narrative or denied agency in historical processes. (In the context of South Asian history this later development took the shape of a revolt against elite history and the emergence of the so-called Subaltern Studies school, named after a series of collections of essays on subaltern themes.)[2] As in other areas of historical writing at the end of the twentieth century, the practice of history in relation to South Asia experienced the erosion of once grand narratives of history— whether of progress and modernization, of the rise of the nation and

the nation-state, or the Marxist narratives of class formation and conflict. Its practitioners were often profoundly influenced by debates on
"discourse," particularly by ideas of "orientalism" which took their inspiration from Edward Said's famous work of that name published
in 1978.[3] A historical view rooted in notions of discourse often drew
historians of South Asia back to older colonial archives that had so recently been decried as elitist, rather than sending them out to search
for new and more illuminating sources. It also belittled the creative
agency of individuals and groups in history, and discouraged proper
attention to the great variety of human experience in different social
and cultural contexts even on one subcontinent. More recently still,
and productively, the history of the subcontinent has begun to be
seen within the matrix of insights that are known loosely as "global
history"—as historians see South Asia as part of complex global networks of trade, investment, migration, education, religion, and ideology. In such a historiographical view South Asian history has to
be studied in its particular geographical context in the Indian Ocean
and through broad themes that tie it to global problems, issues, and
experiences.

I hope that this book will in some measure speak within this complex and one might even say chaotic historiographical context, by
showing how varieties of life histories can illuminate the history of
South Asia and its peoples. Academic historians have in general been
suspicious of biography, deeming it to be a populist form of history
writing, serving an audience that likes its history simple and personal,
rather than being prepared to grapple with underlying historical processes. It is significant that, despite these discontents and despite many
of the larger trends in historiography, in many different fields of history academics have nonetheless turned to varieties of individual and
group biography, in an attempt to find sources with which they can
seek to understand a wide range of historical problems.[4] I do not
see myself as a biographer, though I have written studies that focus
on the lives of prominent individuals such as Mahatma Gandhi and
Jawaharlal Nehru.[5] These do not attempt a minute account of the

life in question from birth to death as the more traditional biographer might. Rather, I attempt to use such individual life histories to probe broad historical themes, and to anchor more theoretical discussions in the lived experiences of real people. Working with life histories can be a nuanced methodology that allows the historian to shift gaze from the general theme and theory to the particular and precise experience of people and groups, moving from one to the another, as each type of focus checks and illuminates the other. Moreover, it is an approach that is particularly productive as we examine some of the issues that deeply concern historians, such as the nature of individual and shared identities and the ways these develop over time in different contexts; the nature of agency in the historical process; and the local and global webs of connection within which people live and work, within and across national boundaries. In the context of the South Asian past, individual lives are also a significant source, particularly in the case of many of those who were prominent in the politics of nationalism and kept their papers for posterity in a conscious attempt to be part of the making of their nation's history. Gandhi and Nehru are but the tip of the iceberg in this respect. Their two and often intertwined lives form the basis for the last two chapters in this book. However, in the first two chapters I suggest that the notion of life history can be expanded beyond that of the individual. Prosopography is of course an established scholarly genre and modus operandi. But in the context of South Asian history I believe that there is much to be gained from moving beyond the study of groups of similar people to a longitudinal study of families (forming the subject of chapter 2) and the study of the life of different sorts of critical institutions, particularly educational ones, not as a throwback to institutional history, but to an examination of the lives moulded by such institutions and their ongoing connections. A case study of this approach is the heart of chapter 1.

There is a further and perhaps more mundane reason for working with life histories as a professional historian. I am concerned with the need to communicate. We work in an age where there has rarely been a greater dichotomy between professional and popular history;

but so often academic historians choose not to address a wider audience or feel that they cannot because of the pressures within academia. We also live in a time when history has rarely been more crucial in the wider public sphere. Lack of historical understanding can lead to huge policy pitfalls. Many would say that at the start of the twenty-first century the governments of the United States and Britain would have benefited from studies in colonial history in Iraq and on the old North West Frontier of India. Moreover, history is central to conflicts and projects of many kinds at the moment. The radical Islamism that is proving so attractive to a younger generation has a particular vision of global religious and cultural history. In India the idea of India and of being Indian is being twisted by a vision of the past which casts Muslims as villains or outsiders. I believe that professional historians cannot just speak to each other and build their careers in a closed self-congratulatory world. They must also be prepared to speak to people of other disciplines and people outside academia. I hope that life histories may be just such an inclusive genre or way of "doing history," and I am most grateful to the University of Notre Dame for giving me this opportunity to explore this historical approach.

CHAPTER I

Colleges, Cohorts, and Dynasties

Our exploration of the potential of new kinds of "life history" which are wider than studies of individuals begins with what I wish to call rather loosely "colleges, cohorts, and dynasties." I want to ask if there are other kinds of "lives" apart from those of individuals which the historian may fruitfully study as a source of evidence about the past. Historians have of course looked at various types of collective lives—career groups or generational groups for example.[1] I want to explore how various kinds of institutions, and educational institutions in particular, have "lives" that can be a real source for the historian, including the historian of South Asia. This is an approach far removed from rather old-fashioned institutional history which tracks the foundation, development, and operation of an institution. Instead it concentrates on the people within them: how they came to be there in the first place, what they learned in the broadest sense, the connections they made there, and where they went subsequently. Schools and colleges not only impart knowledge and train people to think. They also, and often quite intentionally, produce and reproduce specific kinds of people, with common skills and assumptions, and particular sorts of social capital. As such, schools and colleges can become crucial institutions in national and international history and repay a great deal of attention as a historical source.

Historians of different societies have of course recognised this. Those who study Great Britain, for example, have learned much about the significance of the English public schools (in English parlance, those private schools for education in which parents paid fees). From the mid-nineteenth century these were crucial in the creation of a new professional elite in Britain, bound by common educational experiences, assumptions, and beliefs, and new networks of friendship and recognition. They helped to fashion a particular kind of masculinity that was then exported through the British Empire. Indeed British parents whose sons were born in India were determined to send them "home" for schooling from a very early age lest they miss out on this institutional socialisation deemed essential for success as a British upper-class male. The value of this was deemed to outweigh by far the pain of separation felt by both parents and children.[2] It is hardly surprising that historians of empire should have come to see the significance of mechanisms of education and socialisation among the imperial rulers and their subjects. From the English preparatory and public schools, through the Girl Guides and Boy Scouts, to missionary and government schools in the colonies and dependencies, and even the Cambridge Local Examinations Syndicate which ran examinations and awarded school-leaving certificates throughout the empire — all these mechanisms of education in the broadest sense have become grist to the mill of the imperial historian.[3]

Colonial rulers also understood well the key role of educational institutions in the formation of their own kind, and for the new imperial task of forming new generations of key allies in the empire. In India the most obvious example of the latter task was the foundation in the 1870s and 1880s of five schools for the sons of Princes in India, the most famous being Mayo College, Rajasthan, and Aitchison College, Lahore. Here the younger generation of a pre-existing social and political elite were to be educated, disciplined, and modernised in institutions modeled on the English public school, to perform a key role as reinvented "traditional" rulers under the raj. Whether these institutions did what they were supposed to was altogether another matter![4] Aiming to create a rather different level of imperial allies, French imperialists in West Africa at the turn of the twentieth century set up the William Ponty School as a highly selective boarding school off the coast of Senegal for Africans destined to become local schoolmasters, clerks, and medical assistants.[5] Back in India the British authorities, civil and religious, recognised the dangers of *not providing education* for certain groups, particularly the children of mixed race and those of poor European families who could not afford education "at home." In the later nineteenth century the government gave financial help and encouragement to schools for these groups of children, but most were founded and run by churches and religious organisations. As Viceroy Lord Canning had noted in 1860, "If measures for educating these children are not . . . aided by the government, we shall soon find ourselves embarrassed in all large towns and stations with a floating population of Indianized English, loosely brought up, and exhibiting most of the worst qualities of both races." A further consideration was more utilitarian: such institutions would help to instil political loyalty particularly among the children of mixed-race descent and increase their utility as employees of the raj because they were thought to "serve the Government more efficiently than the Natives can . . . and more cheaply and conveniently than Europeans."[6] Creating the right sort of people continued to be a concern even as imperial power ebbed away, though by now the intended products of new foundations were very different: Indian elite children from professional families who were destined to work for a new nation. In the final years of the British raj in India, the Doon School, ironically modeled on the English public schools, was founded by Indians but blessed by the raj as an institution that would produce a certain type of new Indian man and citizen. It is a project that still produces key Indian leaders and reproduces the social capital essential for success in many key areas of postcolonial India.[7]

However, historians of South Asia have paid little attention to key institutions in Britain that played a central role in forging the imperial connections between Britain and India. My own college in Oxford, Balliol College, was perhaps the single most significant of these institutions from the middle of the nineteenth century, after entry into the Indian Civil Service was opened via competitive examination in 1853, thus breaking the stranglehold of patronage by the directors of the East India Company and the domination of the service by families with Company connections and a history of service in India.[8] Luckily for us, Balliol has a remarkable register of its alumni. For the period 1853 to Indian independence in 1947, the period when the competitive entry examination was in place and which I have chosen to examine, these include father's profession and place of residence, schooling, college record, subsequent career, and marriage (including bride's father). Very few other Oxford and Cambridge colleges have such a record. But of those in Oxford that do Balliol had the largest number of its alumni working in the empire from the later nineteenth century to the First World War: 27 percent, and still a substantial number afterwards. Of the Balliol cohorts 1874–75 to 1913–14 who worked in the empire, nearly 60 percent served in India; while 22 percent of the empire-working men served in India even in the leaner years of 1918–19 to 1937–38.[9] I have created a database of all Balliol men of British/European origins who worked in India for most or part of their principal career, and then of all Balliol students of Indian origins in the same period, to show how the life of this particular college and the lives of so many who passed through it are a fascinating and virtually unused source for understanding the many threads of connection between India and Britain in this period.

We first need to know what sort of college Balliol was by the later nineteenth century. Although it was founded in the 1260s, it was not until the early nineteenth century that it achieved its modern character, in terms of financial stability, extended buildings on a core city site, and a powerful academic ethos.[10] It was not an aristocratic college (such as Christ Church) but drew its students from a solid professional social base. It achieved this and raised its intellectual level by the radical move in the late 1820s of opening most of its scholarships to open competitive examination and holding an annual admission of commoners, many of whom came from among those who were runners-up in the scholarship examination. By the next decade these changes were clear in the degree results of its students and it was generally recognised as the foremost intellectual college in the university. One of its greatest Masters was Benjamin Jowett, a radical reformist in many fields, who presided over the college from 1870 to 1893 but was influential as a Fellow for many years before he became Master. He was determined to inculcate hard work and perseverance, the best use of personal talents, and an ideal of public service. This combination turned Balliol into a kindergarten for national and imperial public life. It was soon after his Mastership, in 1908, that the then Prime Minister, H. H. Asquith, himself a Balliol man of the 1870s, spoke of his fellow alumni as being marked by a "tranquil consciousness of effortless superiority."[11] This reflected not just their intellectual prowess, but their increasing influence in many areas of public life — Parliament, the Church, the Civil Service and service in the British Empire. Again it was Jowett who had helped to turn the eyes of so many young men in his college outwards towards the empire, and particularly to India, where two of his brothers had served and died. He corresponded with Florence Nightingale about numerous Indian social and economic issues, and believed that if men wanted to do "great and permanent good" they should go and do it in India.[12] He is reported to have said that he hoped to rule the world through his students; and he played a major role in discussions about entry into the Indian Civil Service once Company patronage had been abolished.

Balliol was not a particularly large college. In 1825 it had just 76 students in residence. This figure rose to 165 in 1885, 183 in 1912, and to nearly 300 in the 1920s and 1930s.[13] Its size makes the number of men of European descent who left to work in India the more remarkable, particularly in the nineteenth century. In the years 1853–1947 there were 345 of them. The numbers began to pick up in the 1860s and became a flood in the later 1870s. (In 1878 there were eighteen entrants to the college who went on to serve in India, and in the 1880 entry there were sixteen.) The numbers tailed off just before the First World War and never recovered. The pattern of occupations is also striking. Two hundred and seventy-three of the total—just over 79 percent—went into the Indian Civil Service. All other professions in India paled into insignificance. Eleven went into the Indian Educational Service, 11 went into various forms of business, 9 went into the Church in India, and another 9 became lawyers. Six went into the Forestry Service, and another 6 into the Indian Army. A solitary Balliol man became a publisher, managing the Bombay branch of Oxford University Press from 1912 to 1923; while another one, clearly a distinguished scientist with a D. Sc. from Edinburgh, became Director of the Indian Museum in Calcutta and eventually Director of the Zoological Survey of India. Balliol also produced three viceroys of India, including Lord Curzon, though they of course were appointed for limited terms of office from Britain rather than being men who made their careers in India.

The fluctuations in the numbers over our period reflect very largely the nature of entry into and preparation for the ICS as well as its degree of popularity for the British professional classes. The abolition of Company patronage and the opening of the ICS to those successful in the competitive examination reflected the wish of the government to have well-educated gentlemen and competent administrators, preferably with a university education, for this largest part of the British Empire. In order to achieve this, and latterly to provide easier access to the competition for Indian candidates, the regulations and the content of the examinations changed somewhat. In the early years of the examination it was expected that men would compete for entry after graduation, but the nature of the examination sent boys off to so-called crammers in London for a better chance of success. So Lord Salisbury as Secretary of State for India contrived a new system which lasted from 1879 to 1892, by which boys took the examination on leaving school and then went to selected universities (of which Oxford took the lion's share) to study for two probationary years subjects considered relevant to their future Indian work, including languages. Partly to accommodate increasing Indian demand for a system that would give them a chance to enter the service, the government subsequently reverted to the system of postuniversity competition, and successful candidates then went for one year to a selected university for training.[14] Throughout these twists and turns of policy Balliol proceeded to produce large numbers of ICS men—more than any other Oxford college, while Oxford itself produced more than any other university. During the so-called Salisbury system of a two-year probationary period, Jowett, who personally favoured a graduate entry and was highly influential in discussions about ICS entry, invited all successful candidates to come to Balliol, and took special care to see they were properly looked after and taught. In 1875, for example, half the ICS probationers in the country were studying in Balliol.[15] This meant that Balliol was sheltering, educating, and socialising twice as many as Cambridge and all the other Oxford colleges put together. The close connection between Balliol and the ICS continued well after this system, not least because the examinations favoured those with Oxford degrees in classics (known as "Greats"). When the content of the examination was being reworked in the early twentieth century it was the Master of Balliol, by then James Strachan Davidson, who was central to the process and helped to ensure that Oxford classicists would be well prepared for the questions![16] Not all the successful Balliol applicants read classics, however: some were orientalists or historians. Nor did they all do particularly well in their degree examinations, though many were high-flyers. Nicholas Beatson Bell, son of an Edinburgh lawyer, came to Balliol in 1886 and gained both a first in Oriental studies and the Boden Scholarship in Sanskrit. He ended his career as Governor of the province of Assam, was

knighted, and ordained into the Church of England the year of his retirement. A later Balliol ICS man, Stuart Abbott, son of an ICS Balliol man, Evelyn R. Abbot, of the 1891 Balliol intake of two-year probationers, who came to Balliol in 1929, achieved a first class in both
parts of his classics degree and passed first in the ICS examination of
his year. For Stuart his father's example must have been particularly
strong, for after the Great War the flow of Balliol men into the ICS
ebbed: in the 1930s only five entered the service. This in turn was part
of a nationwide trend. Numbers of Europeans recruited in the decade
before the war ran between forty in 1912 and fifty-eight in 1906. By the
early 1930s the number was only in the teens and in 1935 dropped to
a dire low of five.[17] This downward trend reflected concerns among
potential applicants and their families about the future of a career in
India,[18] and the growing attraction both of the wider Colonial Service in Africa and the Far East, and the broader range of professions
opening up at home between the wars.

It may be a slight exaggeration to call British rule in India "a Balliol raj," but the numbers were remarkable, and were indeed remarked
on. In 1929 the Balliol-educated Governor of Madras, Lord Goschen,
who was acting as Viceroy, gave a dinner party on 4 September at
Simla, the imperial summer capital, to twenty-seven Balliol men. Between 1916 and 1920 Denys de Saumarez Bray, Balliol 1894–99, was
Deputy Secretary to the Political Department of the Government of
India; two of the more senior Secretaries in the department were
also Balliol men of the 1889 and 1890 vintages. The two older men
would have known each other in college, while Bray overlapped with
the younger of the two. All three were eventually knighted. In fact, of
the Balliol men who worked in India, fifty-eight were knighted, nearly
a quarter of them. This reward for distinguished service (in a service
much concerned with rank and status) reinforces what the college
records indicate: that Balliol men in the ICS rarely remained just district officers, the workhorses of the service. Many more rose high in
the ranks of the administration and concluded their careers in senior
desk jobs in the imperial or provincial capitals. Sir James Meston, for

example (later 1st Baron Meston on his retirement from the ICS), was a lad from Aberdeen in Scotland who came to Balliol from 1883 to 1885 before going into the ICS in the United Provinces in northern India—colloquially known as UP. After becoming an expert in Indian finance he became Lieutenant-Governor of his own province from 1912 to 1917. Sir James Crerar, who went to Balliol as an ICS probationer in 1899–1902 after gaining a first at Edinburgh, was in the later years of his career Secretary to the Home Department of the Government of Bombay, then Secretary to the Home Department, Government of India, and eventually Home Department Member of the Government of India, 1927–32. It fell to him to manage the problem of Gandhi's second civil resistance campaign, after previous experience of the Mahatma in Bombay. Or there was the less fortunate Sir Michael O'Dwyer, an Irishman who was at Balliol from 1882 to 1885. He had a most distinguished career in the northwest of India and ended up as Lieutenant-Governor of the Punjab from 1913 to 1919. Provincial governorships were of course the pinnacle of an ICS career. However, his lieutenant-governorship saw the infamous massacre at Amritsar in 1919 when a British general ordered his troops to fire on an unarmed crowd in a walled space from which there was no easy exit. This episode caught up with him in 1940 in London when he was assassinated, as the college register laconically puts it, "by a fanatic." It might be appropriate at this point to remind ourselves that service in India was not always comfortable or safe, though the material and status rewards were significant. Of the cohorts I have studied sixty-six died unusual or premature deaths—that is just over 19 percent. Two (including O'Dwyer) were assassinated. Three drowned, one died of sunstroke, two were killed by tigers, and six succumbed to fevers of various kinds, particularly smallpox.

But who were our Balliol India hands? What do their social origins and connections tell us about the nature of this linkage between India and Britain, about the people who ruled and worked in India for nearly a century? Like their Balliol contemporaries virtually none of them were aristocrats: they came from solidly professional families.

Their fathers were Anglican or occasionally Free Church clergymen, doctors, lawyers, civil servants at home and in the empire. They were in fact sons of gentlemen. We have already encountered Beatson Bell and Abbott, who were respectively the sons of a lawyer and an ICS man. De Saumarez Bray, whom we met in the Political Department, was the son of a clergyman, while his two senior Balliol colleagues were the sons, respectively, of a clergyman who later became headmaster of Harrow, a famous English public school, and, more unusually, of a baronet. The unfortunate Michael O'Dwyer was something of an oddity, coming from much more modest origins, a Catholic Irish farming family with fourteen children. Not surprisingly, given the role of the public schools in the socialisation of the British professional male in the making, most of them had been to such schools. Bray had been to Blundells in Devon, a school with a long connection with Balliol. His older colleagues had been to Fettes College and to Marlborough. The Abbotts, father and son, had been to Bath College and Rugby. Another father-son Balliol ICS pair, the Kincaids, went to Sherborne and Bradfield respectively. The older Kincaid married the sister of a Balliol contemporary, C. N. Seddon, who also went into the ICS; he had been educated at Liverpool College before Balliol and in turn sent his son to Sherborne, where his brother-in-law had been at school.

The Kincaid-Seddon nexus tells us something more about the Balliol India connection, which was replicated across a much wider range of British people who worked in India. Kipling had written of an earlier time when families sent sons to India generation by generation, like dolphins in a line across the ocean. The patronage networks of the Indian army and the East India Company had reinforced the creation of these Anglo-Indian dynasties. (Here I should say that I use *Anglo-Indian* in its original sense — to mean British people resident in India, not those of mixed descent, who were referred to in the twentieth century as Anglo-Indians. For them I use the clear word *Eurasian*.) Nicholsons, Lawrences, Lyalls, and Stracheys were such dynasties. The Stracheys, a modest landed family from Somerset in the West of England for example, sent thirteen members over four generations to work in India. They were outdone by a Scottish family,

the Lochs, who sent thirty men into Indian service over four successive generations, six in the Civil Service, and many of the rest in the
army.[19] Familial connections with India, and interlocking marriages between families with such connections, remained a significant feature
of the British connection with India. In Balliol's case this was often
reinforced by membership of the college over several generations of
a family's males, and by marriage connections with similar Balliol-
India families. Coming from later generations and very different societies, we need to recognise that quite apart from the India connection
the role of a man's Oxbridge college in the formation of families over
several generations and in their extended networks through marriage
and friendship tended to be very important. This is perhaps not unex-
pected when one considers the small size of the British professional
elite and the limited numbers of public schools and colleges to which
they went. It is very clear from the Balliol registers. The younger Abbott of the 1929 Balliol intake had a father, uncle, and great-uncle
at Balliol. He in turn married the daughter of a Balliol man; she was
also the sister of two of his near contemporaries at Balliol. This was
a match that must have been made if not in Balliol, when she would
have visited her brothers, at least through the Balliol connection.
(They in turn sent one of their sons to Balliol in 1958. This young man
therefore had seven Balliol men in his close ancestry.)

If we look at the 345 Balliol men who served in India of the
1853–1947 intakes, the family and matrimonial links with other British families working in India are most striking. Seventy of them had
family connections with India through their own natal families. Thirty-
four married women with similar Indian connections. Another fourteen had both natal and matrimonial connections with Anglo-Indian
families. This means that just over 34 percent of Balliol men who
worked in India were linked to that subcontinent via different and
often multiple family connections—making the raj in its broadest
sense something of a family business as well as a career linked with a
particular type of education at school and university. This also tells us
much about the place of India in the mental picture and professional
and social experience of a key elite in British society. Let me take some

examples to put flesh and blood on these bald statistics. First there were those with both natal and matrimonial connections with India. One of the Loch family, the Anglo-Indian dynasty dating back to Company days, arrived in Balliol in 1864, gaining a second in classics part 1 and then a second in history and law. This young Loch, Willie Walker Loch, was the son of George, a Calcutta High Court judge, and in 1868, by now in the ICS in Bombay, he married the daughter of another ICS man. (While I was preparing the lectures on which this book is based, the great-great-nephew of Willie Walker Loch wrote to me. He himself had come to Balliol in 1964 and now offered me a copy of the original covenant Willie Walker Loch had signed when he entered the ICS in 1868. It is reproduced as figure 1 a–c. He wanted a good home for it because, as he told me, he had been born in India as had both his parents. His grandfathers had both worked in the Indian Medical Service. History comes alive if you are in the right place at the right time!) Another example from a dynasty of Anglo-Indians who spread over several generations was Frederick Augustus Hugh Elliot, who was educated at Harrow and was at Balliol from 1866 to 1868. He went into the ICS in Bombay, following in the Indian footsteps of his father, who had been Chief Presidency Magistrate in Madras, and of his grandfather (a Balliol man of 1768), who had been Governor of Madras. Frederick in turn married the daughter of Surgeon-Major Elijah Impey, working in Bombay. Other Balliol men belonged to similar families. Francis Sladen, educated at Charterhouse and Balliol, went into the ICS in 1899, following his father's career.[20] The Kincaid family sent three generations of men to India: William, who had been Resident of Bhopal State; his son Charles, Balliol 1889–91, who went into the ICS in Bombay Presidency; and his son, Dennis, Balliol 1924–28, who also went into the ICS in Bombay. The youngest Kincaid drowned in 1937 at the age of thirty-two at the beach in Kanara, the place to which he had recently been posted as Sessions Judge. He is intriguing as well as tragic. He had only gained a fourth in his final degree exams in classics (a class not possible today), but he was clearly a literary man of note, and in his short life wrote eight books (all

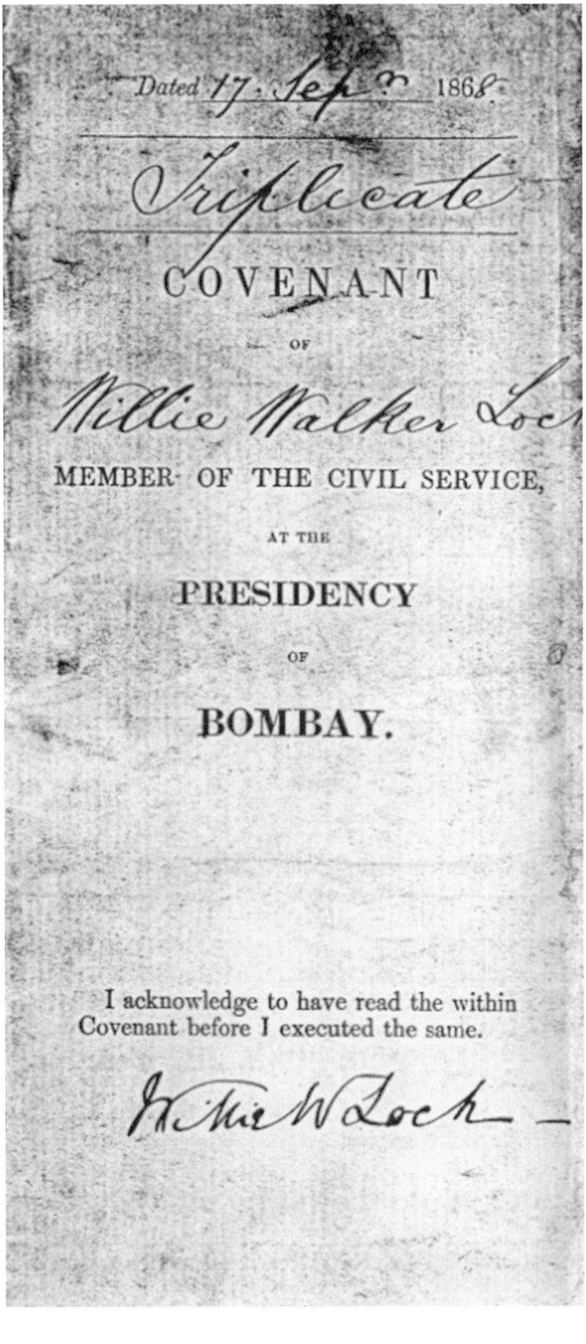

Dated *17 Sep* 186*8*

Triplicate

COVENANT

OF

Willie Walker Loch

MEMBER OF THE CIVIL SERVICE,

AT THE

PRESIDENCY

OF

BOMBAY.

I acknowledge to have read the within Covenant before I executed the same.

Willie W Loch

Figure 1 a–c.
The covenant signed
by W. W. Loch
(Balliol, 1864–67)
when he entered
the ICS in 1868.
Courtesy of the
Rev. Hamish Fullerton,
great-great-nephew
of Willie Walker Loch.

This Indenture made the *seventeenth* day of *September* in the year of our Lord 186*8*, between *Willie Walker Lock* herein-after called the Covenantor of the one part, and the Secretary of State in Council of the other part. Whereas the said Secretary of State in Council has appointed the Covenantor to serve Her Majesty as a member of the Civil Service of India at and to belong to the Presidency of Bombay in the East Indies, such service to continue during the pleasure of Her Majesty, Her heirs and successors, to be signified under the hand of the Secretary of State for India, but with liberty for the said Covenantor to resign the said service, with the previous permission of the Secretary of State in Council or of the Governor in Council of the said Presidency. Now this Indenture witnesseth, and the said Covenantor doth hereby covenant and agree with and to the said Secretary of State in Council, in manner and form following; that is to say,— *[margin: Recital of the terms on which the party enters into the service.]* *[margin: He covenants,]*

1st. That while he shall be employed in the said service he will faithfully, honestly, and diligently do all such things as shall be lawfully committed to his charge by or on the part of the Secretary of State in Council, or of the Government in India, or in execution of his duty. *[margin: For his general fidelity.]*

2nd. That he will perform and obey all such general rules and regulations of the Secretary of State in Council and of the said service as shall be in force in relation to all things to be committed to his charge or to be done by him, or to any rank, office, or station in which he shall act, and will observe and obey all such orders relating to himself or his conduct as he shall receive from the Secretary of State in Council, or the Governor in Council of the said Presidency, or any person who shall have lawful authority to command him. *[margin: To obey orders of a general nature, and especially relating to the party.]*

3rd. That he will regularly and justly keep all accounts touching his transactions for the Government in India, and will preserve and keep all such documents, chattels, and realty as shall be committed to his charge, or as it shall be his duty to preserve and keep, and shall not wilfully obliterate, cancel, or injure, nor permit to be obliterated, cancelled, or injured, any documents, chattels, or realty belonging to Her Majesty, or in the custody of any person or persons on account of the Government, and will deliver all such documents, chattels, and realty as shall be in his custody or power to any person to whom he ought to deliver the same. And on demand made by or on behalf of the Secretary of State in Council, or of the Government of the said Presidency, will deliver to such person or persons as shall be authorized to demand the same, all documents whatsoever touching any of the affairs or concerns of the Government, or anything in which he shall have been engaged as a servant in the Civil Service of India; such delivery to be made without obliteration or concealment of any part of the books, papers, or writings to be delivered up, and notwithstanding that they may not be the property of Her Majesty, or that there may be any entry or entries relating to his own affairs or those of any other person, or any other reason whatever. *[margin: To keep regular accounts, to preserve and duly deliver over chattels and realty, and to produce private accounts.]*

4th. That he shall not make use of or apply the property of Her Majesty which he may have for any purposes other than those for which he ought to use and apply it in the course of his said service, save and except such furniture, goods, and chattels as he may be justly entitled to the use of for his own proper accommodation. *[margin: Not to misapply or employ for improper purposes the property intrusted to his care.]*

5th. That he shall not nor will divulge, disclose, or make known any matter relating to the affairs or concerns of the Government in India, or relating to any matter or thing in which he may act or be concerned or which may come to his knowledge in the course of his said service which may require secrecy, and which ought to be kept secret (save and except as his duty may require), unless he shall be authorized or required to disclose and make known the same by the Secretary of State in Council or the Governor in Council of the said Presidency, or some other person or persons having competent authority for that purpose. *[margin: Not to divulge secrets.]*

6th. That he shall not at any time, directly or indirectly, ask, demand, accept, or receive any sum of money, or security for money, or other valuable thing or service whatsoever, or any promise or engagement by way of present, gift, or gratuity, from any person or persons with whom or on whose behalf he shall, on the part of the Government of India, have any dealings or transactions, business or concern whatsoever, or from any person or persons from whom, by law or any orders or regulations of the Secretary of State in Council, or of any of the branches of the Government in India, he is or shall be restrained from demanding or receiving any sum of money or other valuable thing as a gift or present, or under colour thereof. *[margin: Not to accept corrupt presents, or make corrupt bargains.]*

7th. That he shall not nor will by himself, or in partnership with any other person or persons, or by the agency of any other person or persons, either as principal, factor, or agent, directly or indirectly engage, carry on, or be concerned in any trade, bank, dealings, or transactions whatsoever. *[margin: Not to trade contrary to law or regulations.]*

(4109.)

Figure 1 b.

2

Not to quit India without leave, and to satisfy all debts to Her Majesty before departure.	8th. That he shall not nor will at any time return to Europe, nor remove from or leave the said Presidency without the previous permission of the Governor in Council of the said Presidency in writing; and previously to any such return or removal he shall pay, satisfy, and perform all such debts, sums of money, duties, and engagements as he shall owe or be liable to perform to Her Majesty or to the Government of India, or any branch or department of the same.
To become a subscriber to the Civil Fund and the Annuity Fund.	9th. That he shall and will forthwith upon his arrival at the said Presidency become a subscriber to the Civil Fund and the Annuity Fund there, and shall and will from time to time, so long as he shall continue in the said service, conform to all the rules and regulations which shall be in force in relation to the said funds respectively, and will pay such subscriptions as, under such rules and regulations, shall from time to time become due or payable by him, or at the option of the said Secretary of State in Council or of the Governor in Council of the said Presidency, allow the amount of such subscriptions to be deducted out of any money due or payable by the Government to him.

In witness whereof, the said Covenantor and *R. D. Mangles, Esquire,* and *Sir Frederick Currie, Baronet*

being two members of the Council of India, have hereunto set their hands and seals, the day and year first above written.

Signed, sealed, and delivered by the above named *Willie Walker Loch*

in the presence of *Arthur Hobhouse*

Signed, sealed, and delivered by the above named *R. D. Mangles Esq* and *Sir F Currie* being two members of the Council of India, in the presence of *Fredk. Trevor*

Figure 1 c.

of them while in the ICS) including three novels, an account of the Mahratta hero Shivaji, and a serious work, *British Social Life in India, 1608–1937,* published the year after he died.

It is perhaps not surprising that well over eighty of our Balliol-India men (just over 23 percent) married women whose fathers worked in India. They would have gone to India as young men in their early twenties and would have naturally gravitated to the daughters of senior British men working in India. They had few other options in India apart from young unmarried British women with matrimonial intentions who tended to visit relatives in the annual cold weather. (They were known rather unkindly as "the fishing fleet"; while those who left for home without a prospective husband were more cruelly called "returned empties.") If these two sources did not yield up possible wives, the young European ICS man would have had to wait four years or more for his first home leave to find a bride at home. It was virtually unthinkable at that time that they would marry an Indian or Eurasian girl, particularly if they were in government service. Francis Sladen's photographs of India, now in the college library, show the creation of a very British domesticity by an ICS family. The one reproduced as figure 2 shows the drawing room of a bungalow, and we can see how the British domestic scene is reproduced with an Indian twist—as with the skin of a game trophy draped over the grand piano, or the old-fashioned punkah (fan) operated by ropes in the days before electricity and ceiling fans, hanging over furniture and furnishings designed as far as possible to recreate the known domesticity of "home" in England. It is significant that in the foreground the chair has a cushion whose cover has on it the Oxford University crest and motto *Dominus Illuminatio Mea* (The Lord My Light). Such a photograph would have been taken both as a record and to show relatives in England. British social life in India was bounded by strict conventions that served to police the boundaries of intimacy between British and Indian, particularly across the sexes, and to reproduce as far as possible upper-middle-class British life in an alien land, focused on the club and the bungalow, which were until very late in the raj inhospitable to Indians except as servants.[21] Figure 3 shows the wife and children of one of Sladen's colleagues, and the large retinue of their domestic servants required to keep them in the manner in which British officials believed they should live, in order to keep up European domestic standards and to set an example of domestic order and cleanliness. (We can even see in the front right the *darzi* [tailor] with his sewing machine; and to the front left the only female servant, the *ayah,* who would have helped to look after the children. In front of her sits the family's pet dog—the replication of yet another aspect of British domestic life!) It is a photo that is replicated in thousands of family albums belonging to British people who worked in India under the raj.

Figure 2. British domestic interior, UP, India, 1901–2. From the Sladen photograph albums, Balliol College archives.

The Balliol records have shown how a virtually unused source generated by the life history of a key educational institution, and a study of the cohorts of undergraduates who passed through it, can yield up many insights into the nature of British interests in and connections with India in the days of imperial rule. In particular it reveals the very large and close-knit group, linked together by educational experience and assumptions about their rightful place as public servants, by social background, friendship, and marriage, who manned the key services of the raj, particularly the ICS. They were in turn part

Figure 3. Wife and children of J. H. Cox, Deputy Commissioner of Hardoi and senior ICS colleague of F. Sladen (Balliol, 1894–99). They are shown in front of their bungalow with their retinue of servants, c. 1903. From the Sladen photograph albums, Balliol College archives.

of a increasingly dominant elite in British social and political life, and their "Indian interest" explains some of the worth of India to Britain at least until the First World War. The "worth of India" to Britain encompassed of course trade, investment, and the empirewide security that flowed from control of the Indian army and key Asian seaways. But the career and emotional connections with India of this elite, of whom Balliol men were a key part, was also a significant element in British attitudes to the Indian empire. It also suggests that the ebbing of these connections after the Great War, so vividly displayed in the Balliol experience, may in part account for the rapid end of that empire in the middle of the twentieth century.

Balliol's life history includes another important element in its connections with India: namely those Indians who came to study in Oxford. For our purposes I have limited my research to those who entered the college between 1853 and 1947, the opposite flow to those men we have just been considering. In this period eighty-eight Indian students studied at Balliol. The majority were Hindus, reflecting the demographic majority on the subcontinent. About 20 percent were Muslim, rather less than their proportion of the Indian population, and a handful were Sikhs and Parsis. There were at the time very few permanent Indian residents in Britain, and the Balliol Indians were all from the subcontinent itself—unlike today of course when a student with an Indian name may well be born and brought up in the UK. All those who came to Oxford and other universities from India undertook an enormous enterprise in coming to study in Britain. It was not just a very serious financial investment; for there were few scholarships. It meant prolonged separation from family, and managing huge cultural adjustments in such matters as climate, living conditions, food, and personal relationships, as well as patterns of study.[22] Again in Balliol's life it was Master Benjamin Jowett who really made the college a welcoming place for Indian students. While he was Master forty-nine Indians came to the university as a whole, and twenty-two of these came to Balliol.[23] He also notably befriended the sister of one of his Indian Balliol men. Cornelia Sorabji was at Somerville College in the early 1890s and was sister to Richard (at Balliol 1890–93): they were the children of a Christian Indian clergyman, whose family had originally been Parsi. Jowett invited her into the college for social occasions, mentored her academically and introduced her to many luminaries of British public and intellectual life. Both Sorabjis went on to become lawyers, Cornelia becoming India's first woman barrister.[24] Jowett's Mastership was probably the time when the Indian presence in Balliol was one of the bones of contention between the college and its next-door neighbour, Trinity. (It is said that Trinity men would shout ironically across the shared wall, "Bring out your white man.")[25] Only a trickle of the eighty-eight men we are considering came before Jowett's Mastership, but thereafter there was a small but steady flow of one or two a year. The flow really gathered pace between the world wars, just at the time when the reverse stream was ebbing and fewer Balliol men of British origin were choosing India as their place of work. Four Indians came in 1927 and the same number in 1931, for example. What is significant and perhaps ironic is that this was just the time when the nationalist movement had really become a profoundly significant force in India, and its major leader, Gandhi, had severe reservations about education in English and British-controlled institutions, and was urging noncooperation with British rule and a return to an earlier rural civilisation. However, the parents who invested in their sons' (and very rarely their daughters') education in England at this time recognised its worth for them and their whole families in terms of status and later long-term careers and earning power. Like their British Balliol counterparts, most of the Indian students at Balliol came from professional families, particularly those of lawyers, who had the financial resources to enable foreign travel and study for several years. Their children would of course already have had an English medium education. (By the mid- to late nineteenth century there were elite schools and colleges offering an English education in India; very unusually, as in the case of Jawaharlal Nehru, who attended Harrow School in London before Cambridge, an Indian boy would be sent to school in England.) Balliol Indians also came from a wide geographical spread rather than being a regional cluster of, for example, Bengalis, who had early on been dominant in English-language education in India. There was a rare Balliol Indian who came from a major landholding or princely family—though the Baroda and Kapurthala royal families, for example, did send young men to Balliol. Of those who came to Balliol in these years, thirty-one went into the ICS, just 35 percent of the total. Twenty-one became lawyers—that is nearly 24 percent of the total. Thirteen became educationalists and academics. One, the Nawab of Pataudi, at Balliol from 1927 to 1931, was not only a princely ruler but famously played cricket for Oxford and then after he had left Balliol for England. (His son, also a Balliol man but of a postindependence vintage [1959–63], captained Oxford at cricket for two years and then went on to captain India through the 1960s and at the same time captained the English county of Sussex.)

The presence of this significant cohort of Indians in Balliol tells us something about the ethos and cosmopolitan nature of the college, and the fact that British Balliol men going to India would in their formative years have had occasion to meet as equals Indians of a similar social background. It should be recognised that this did not extend to social intimacy in India itself across the racial divide except that particular form of comradeship possible between men of equal class and professional status who worked together in the same offices, departments, or courts. Notions of racial difference and inequality, intertwined with those of class and practices of outright racism, were prevalent right up to independence. Indeed, the last Viceroy, Lord Mountbatten, made the ending of social discrimination on racial grounds a key part of his strategy of ending the raj with a semblance of grace and good will. He threatened to send home immediately anyone heard making racist remarks, and all social occasions over which he and Lady Mountbatten presided included an unprecedented number of Indians. Far more important was the contribution being part of Balliol's life history made to these Indian alumni in achieving status and prominent roles in Indian public life. Those who became civil servants, lawyers, and academics were pioneers in the earlier generations, and they and their successors became part of a new professional elite in Indian public life, gaining professional and eventually political status, as well as the material rewards that went with their professions.

Those who graduated from the 1930s were a particularly favoured generation. Many of them received unusually rapid promotion after independence, as more senior British people, particularly in the ICS, left the country, thereby opening up the career ladder to competent young aspirants.[26] Moreover, independent India needed people to fill new roles, particularly in the new Foreign Service. Balliol men were there ready and waiting! Let us take one or two examples. Venkata Viswanathan from Bangalore came to Balliol in 1930–31 and thence into the ICS in UP. He was wending his way up the career ladder when independence came, offering him unheard-of opportunity. He went to Pakistan as Deputy High Commissioner at independence, then held senior posts in central India, before going to Delhi to work in senior positions in the Home Ministry of the Government of India. He spent two years as Chief Commissioner of Delhi and then hit the high spots becoming in succession Lieutenant-Governor of Himachal Pradesh and then Governor of Kerala state. A younger Balliol man, G. Narain, from UP, who was at Balliol 1939–40, went immediately back to the ICS in his home province after Oxford. Within nine years he was Secretary to the Home Department of the UP government— a hugely accelerated promotion. He became the state's Chief Secretary within another decade and then went on to senior posts in the Government of India. Others found that the new Foreign Service offered scope for their talents and a rapid rise. H. Tyabji, of a notable Bombay Muslim family, came to Balliol in 1931–32. Two of his uncles and a cousin had also been at Balliol. He married into Balliol in a way as well, as his wife was the niece of his Balliol cousin! He too went into the ICS. Transferring to the new Indian Foreign Service in 1948 he was within six years an ambassador, ending his career in 1967 after two years as Ambassador to Japan. B. K. Nehru, Balliol 1933–34, made his mark as an economics specialist in the Government of India. He had done an economics degree at the London School of Economics before Balliol. He also became an ambassador—to Washington in 1961—and then a state governor in 1968. K. S. Singh from the Punjab, who was at Balliol 1938–39 went into the ICS in 1939, transferred to the Foreign Service and soon reached ambassadorial level. He was Deputy High Commissioner in London from 1962 to 1965, then became High Commissioner to Pakistan in 1965 and Ambassador to the USSR in 1967. Balliol therefore continued to make its mark in India well after independence, and in India's worldwide presence, through the careers of men who had come to Oxford in the closing years of the raj.

In this chapter I have expanded the historical technique of "life history" to focus on the life of an educational institution, and, as a historian of South Asia, to probe what the records of the lives of its cohorts of alumni at a particular period can tell us about linkages between India and Britain, and about the characteristics of those who sustained the British imperial presence in India. The role of Balliol in fashioning so many of the British men who ruled India through the ICS is particularly striking. So are the numerous interconnections of these men as part of an Anglo-Indian elite within the British ruling class. The kinship and marriage connections between them, often rooted in the subcontinent as well as the college, have led me to consider them as Anglo-Indian "dynasties." The college records also show how Balliol was a magnet and powerful force in Indian lives as well, particularly after the First World War. This was ironic as it was just the time when Gandhi was urging his compatriots to withdraw their cooperation from the raj and its institutions, including its schools and colleges. After 1947 many of those associated with Gandhi in the nationalist movement did reap the political fruits of independence as political leaders and parliamentarians at the national and state level. But in the *governance* of the country many of those who had taken the opportunities of cooperation with British rule, and service within it, also came into their own, running the domestic administration and moulding their successors in their own imperial image, making up the new Foreign Service and representing their country abroad, often achieving high positions and personal success.

This chapter has underlined the importance of family links as well as college affiliation and experience. Particularly among the British Balliol men we have noted how family experiences and ties with India were of profound significance. The family is the link with the next chapter. For I want to ask if historians, and particularly historians of South Asia, could fruitfully use the life histories of whole families to deepen their understanding of the history of the subcontinent and its peoples.

CHAPTER 2

Family Histories

The previous chapter examined aspects of the "life history" of a particular Oxford college, to ask whether they could provide new source material for the historian of South Asia. The personal and career records of Balliol men who served in India demonstrated, among many other things, considerable evidence about the significance of British family traditions and connections in the creation of a professional elite involved with imperial India. This provided a perspective rather different from existing work on imperial families through the lens of their management of childhood when far away from home.[1] This chapter turns to South Asian families as the focus. In particular I want to ask whether what I call the longitudinal study of families could be a historical technique for a deeper understanding of social change over several generations of South Asians. My hope is that this may be a means of opening a window on to the lives of those who often do not leave behind written records, such as those convention-ally used by historians, particularly women and those many who mi-grated from the subcontinent from the early nineteenth century. So in a sense this is a search for a way of encountering and listening to "subaltern" lives—to use the terminology that has informed much writing on South Asia since the early 1980s. But this is only the start of a project, just a sketch of what might be a fruitful mode of histori-cal research. I hope it may address the twin problems of sources and communication outside the often closed world of academic history.

At the outset it is worth remembering that here exists one of the greatest gulfs between popular and academic history. Family history has probably never been as popular as it is today because we increas-ingly live in a highly mobile society, where many people and their an-cestors have moved through choice or compulsion of different sorts. People of many kinds are searching for their roots, whether these lie in slavery, in recent large-scale migrations, or in the more prosaic resi-dence of families in one area over many generations. Modern tech-nology has made this far more possible and less laborious, particu-larly as various kinds of official demographic records have become accessible on the Internet. Certificates of births, marriages, and deaths, details of census records over a hundred years old, and records of those killed in the two world wars of the past century have all opened up to people, at least in the Western world, details of their relatives' experiences which would once have taken months of painstaking re-search in many different record repositories, and would in many cases have required foreign travel. Moreover, television programme mak-ers have realised that the personal journeys of ancestral discovery make dramatic and fascinating viewing, showing what complex mix-tures most of us are, and often how chequered was the experience of our ancestors.[2] This sort of popular family history is by its very na-ture quite limited and often fails to move beyond amateur genealogy. It also remains the case that the evidence uncovered can often only be interpreted if one already knows a considerable amount about so-cial history, particularly about the lives and conventions of particular social and regional groups, the opening of new economic opportunities, or the economic disasters that have driven people away from home in search of a living, or the political pressures that have displaced many hundreds of thousands. Professional historians, by comparison with enthusiastic amateurs, have shown comparatively little interest in family history. An exception is the case of elite and colourful dynasties such as the British Strachey family.[3]

In relation to South Asia, family history is particularly difficult, given the absence of the sort of personal records generated in Europe and America by the recording requirements of the modern state in relation to its citizens. To this day many South Asians, particularly those of rural origin, have no certificates of key life events—a fact which makes life profoundly difficult when they come up against the bureaucratic formalities of migration. Moreover, the decennial census, straight descendent of the colonial census in India, does not provide the sort of household information available in the underlying records of the British census, for example. There are of course for higher-caste Hindu families the religious records of births, deaths, and marriages kept by a family priest at holy sites such as Banares or Hardwar; and a member of at least one such family has written a delightful memoir of three generations of his family's life.[4] Some historians of the subcontinent have recognised the importance of retrieving family history, or of contributing to the historical record with memoirs of their own families. Antoinette Burton, for example, professor of history at the University of Illinois, has made available in a modern edition a family history written by the daughter of one of India's earliest nationalist leaders and the first president of the Indian National Congress.[5] Elizabeth Buettner has contributed greatly to our knowledge of British families in India, of the sort we encountered in chapter 1, in her *Empire Families: Britons and Late Imperial India.*[6] A Fijian Indian, now professor of history at the Australian National University, has opened up the world of indentured labourers in late nineteenth-century Fiji with an examination of his own grandfather's experience in a most moving way, and with his personal engagement with what he has called his own "unwritten past."[7] Other historians have focused on particular issues in family life rather than on the life histories of particular families, in the rich emerging literature on gender in colonial India. Dealing with the public world there is a significant corpus of writing on gender and nationalism. Examining the private world there is important work on the development of a Victorian Indian domesticity on the subcontinent, including the changing nature of the marital relationship and the expected role of the good Indian woman.[8]

However, if we hope to use the life history of particular families over several generations as a historical source, particularly for the experience of women and those who took their lives in their hands and made the journey overseas, what sources might we be able to use? There are occasionally the personal and family memoirs I have just noted. A newer and developing literary genre was that of autobiography. There are significant numbers of autobiographies that Indians began to write from the late nineteenth century, experimenting with a new way of writing that tried to reflect and make sense of the changing times and intellectual environment in which they were living. Of course anybody who could write such a work whether in English or a regional vernacular, was to an extent a member of the educated elite, given the low levels of literacy until well into the twentieth century. Even in the early 1920s only 17 percent of adult males were literate and a tiny 2 percent of adult women. Moreover, most autobiographies were written for very different purposes than to record family history, as Javed Majeed has recently demonstrated.[9] Gandhi, for example, wrote his autobiography in serial form as a didactic mechanism for the readers of one of his newspapers in the mid-1920s. He was well aware that he was engaging with a literary form that was thought to be Western rather than really Indian. But he insisted that he was not attempting "a real autobiography," but rather a highly selective account of his life to date in order to share with his readers in numerous experiments, social, moral, spiritual, political, and dietary, as he pursued the goal of a vision of Truth. He actually subtitled it "The Story of My Experiments with Truth."[10]

Nonetheless it contains vignettes that tell us much about the life of his fairly conservative middle-class family from what is now Gujarat, in western India. We see him married at the age of thirteen, as was usual; and as a child husband reading cheap, popular pamphlets on marriage and conjugal love, amongst other social issues. We read of him trying unsuccessfully to teach his illiterate child bride to read. Or again, when he prepared to go as a student to England to study law, we hear how his widowed mother agreed to let him go, amidst a storm of caste protest, provided he swore a sacred oath not to touch wine, women, and meat. The autobiographies of Jawaharlal Nehru and his sister, Vijayalakshmi, tell us much about a far wealthier and more Westernised household in Allahabad, where their father, Motilal, was one of India's most successful lawyers and was able to sustain a lifestyle the envy of most British people working in India. They lived in the European part of town for a start. Their house was huge, with two kitchens, one for Indian food and one for European. They had their own swimming pool and riding ring. Motilal financed his son at Harrow School in London and then Trinity College, Cambridge, followed by the Inns of Court. Such privilege and opportunity was perhaps natural for the only son and heir, who, it was hoped, would be a candidate for the ICS. (The young Nehru did not get a first class at Cambridge and decided instead of the ICS to read for the bar. Later in life he pondered ironically on what he had escaped!) Perhaps more interestingly, Motilal engaged a private governess for his two daughters, at a time when there were few elite schools for girls in India, and to send girls to England for schooling was almost unheard of. Motilal mixed with the British and Indian elite of the United Provinces, in northern India, inviting as his guest the Lieutenant-Governor of the province as easily as the Kashmiri Brahmins of his own community. His young son would peep from behind a curtain at these convivial male gatherings in their home. As he recorded, what he saw was sometimes a revelation. "Once I saw him drinking claret or some other red wine. Whisky I knew. I had often seen him and his friends drink it. But this new red stuff filled me with horror and I rushed to my mother to tell her that father was drinking blood."[11]

The somewhat older Cornelia Sorabji, pioneering Oxford student in the early 1890s, and sister of a Balliol man, whom we encountered in chapter 1 as a protégée of Jowett, Master of Balliol, also wrote about her life, particularly her legal work for women in purdah. But the first chapter gives a glimpse into her home life, as the daughter of a Parsi convert to Christianity. Their homes were bungalows such as the British inhabited in India, and like those of other Parsi families they were furnished in Victorian English style. They ate in the English way (off plates, and with knives and forks rather than their fingers), and therefore travel to England held no cultural horrors and confusions as it did for the young Gandhi.[12]

Insights into household space and arrangements can tell the historian much about the division of space and labour within a family, particularly illuminating for gender roles and relations. As Nehru hinted, even in that most modern of Indian households at the start of the twentieth century there were distinct areas for men and women, particularly for entertaining guests, and the Indian kitchen prepared the food that the more orthodox older women of the household considered appropriate and congenial. Nehru's mother would almost certainly never have joined in the male socialisation over alcohol and cigarettes. However, she did attend the 1911 Delhi Durbar with her husband as the guest of the province's Lieutenant-Governor. Further evidence on the use of domestic space and the roles of women in the new form of urban household can be found in the new genre of didactic literature for women appearing from the early part of the nineteenth century. Written in various regional vernaculars, they aimed to teach women how to be good wives, mothers, and housewives in a changing social world, where women had to learn to behave in ways appropriate as wives of educated and often professionally mobile men, and where there might no longer be older female residents of a joint household to manage or indeed dominate the way the home was run.[13] Another written source of a rather different kind is of course creative literature, particularly the novel or short story with its assumptions about the South Asian household and its wider social setting. Of course many of these were written in vernacular languages, and only a few have been translated into English.[14] However, the imaginative literature generated by migration overseas means that novels in English about South Asians in the worldwide diaspora are far more accessible to a wide audience. I need hardly detail any of these, but there are of course V. S. Naipal's pioneering novels on Indians in the Caribbean, while more recently Monica Ali has illuminated in her controversial *Brick Lane* (2003) the confusions and challenges of being a Bangladeshi bride in the East End of London.

Historians do not have to rely only on written historical sources of various kinds. Photography came to India in the mid-nineteenth century, and very soon families, amongst other groups, as well as individuals, were using the new form of visual recording and communication for their own distinctive ends, as Indian photographic studios opened up to serve this new clientele.[15] Having photographs taken was for those Indian families who could afford it, not just a way of recording key events and people; it was also a visual mechanism for establishing the family's status and what they wished to portray about themselves. It was in many ways a mini-dramatic production, taking time and investment, and elaborate direction by the photographer in his studio, determining the poses of the family members to display their status and relationships, and surrounding the subjects with appropriate props. In this Indians were of course very similar to their Western counterparts who were consumers of this new form of recorded image, though some of the messages they wished to convey may been different. We have seen in chapter 1 an example of how imperial families in India used amateur photography to record for themselves and their relatives the domestic details of British lives in India. Just as in England or America, the Indian family soon invested in images other than the family or wedding group, including maturing children who completed higher education and were photographed at graduation. So much historical evidence is present in this early photography, for those with eyes to see — whether it be status with an extended family, the degree of "reform" in dress and gender relations the family wished to project, the nature of the marriage relationship, childhood, and young adulthood. (Later of course Indian politicians also began to realise the importance of photography for their public image at home and abroad—though this is a rather different subject, and to spend time on it would mean a considerable intellectual detour!)

Let us think about several examples of family photography and how the historian might read them.[16] In the Nehru Memorial Library in New Delhi a vast photographic section houses a visual record of Nehru from childhood to his death. One of the earliest photos was taken in 1894, when he was five years old (see fig. 4). It is a set piece of photography with mother, father, and young son posed in front of a screen and several potted plants. The young mother sits rather uncomfortably and uneasily on a chair, wearing what is obviously a best sari; while her young son sits beside her on another chair dressed in some sort of military- or naval-inspired suit with long trousers and boots, looking straight at the photographer with a confident and inquisitive eye. The successful lawyer and paterfamilias stands protectively behind them, clearly dominating the little group, wearing the European fashion of the day, with a winged collar and a pocket watch hanging from a chain on his waistcoat. Given the fair complexions of the Kashmiri Brahmins, almost the only indication that they are Indian is the mother's clothing and hairstyle. The photo not only indicates the flavour of the family relationships among the three of them, it says without words, "Look at us, a modern, Westernised nuclear family. Look at our clothes and our demeanor—we have made ourselves a success in the new India." Rather different, but equally making a major cultural statement is a photograph in the memoirs of my former colleague, Professor Tapan Raychaudhuri, whose family were landowners in East Bengal before the partition of 1947 (see fig. 5). In this photograph, which dates from the late nineteenth century in Bengal and is almost contemporary with the formal photograph of the Nehru family, his grandfather as a young man relaxes on the floor in Bengali dress with his new bride on the floor beside him, leaning

Figure 4. The Nehru family, 1894. Courtesy of the Nehru Memorial Library, New Delhi.

Figure 5. Grandparents of Professor Tapan Raychaudhuri, formerly Reader in Indian History, University of Oxford, c. 1895. Courtesy of Professor Tapan Raychaudhuri.

endearingly against him, with their arms interlocked. The choice of posture says that this is that unusual relationship for the time—a love match. It would not seem out of place a century later but was certainly most unusual for its day, and strikingly different from the many stiff and formal poses adopted in wedding photographs where the couples' body language suggests they were virtual strangers (which of course they often were).[17] Furthermore, the choice of dress and posture in this Bengali photograph perhaps also proclaims a proud Bengali identity, in contrast to the Nehru claim to Western modernity.

However, apart from the ways historians can use these various records and images, another way into "doing history" through family lives is to approach living family members and ask key questions about their particular families alongside the construction of a family tree. This is not oral history as such, which asks living informants for their memories, and has developed into a distinct genre of historical research.[18] It is instead a strategy for getting at important aspects of social change through the record of significant aspects of a family's life which are traced for successive generations. Let me suggest how this could be done, in relation to the two groups I noted at the start of this lecture—South Asian women and migrants—both of which are groups who for lack of education and opportunity are less likely to have left behind many written records.

Let us start with the experience of women in South Asia. There has been a huge blossoming of historical research on the lives and experiences of women on the subcontinent over at least three decades. Initially this was a feminist project to retrieve the history of half the population of the subcontinent which had been submerged by older historical writing, which relied almost entirely on records generated by a male imperial raj and its key male collaborators, opponents and interlocutors.[19] Quite quickly such research came to be seen as not just contributing to "women's history," but to be an integral part of a far broader historical understanding of the significance of gender as fundamental to the ideology and practice of imperialism and to the emergence of nationalism and the new nation-states of the subcontinent.[20] As a result of such scholarship we know much about the broad trends that have transformed the lives of many (but not all) women on the subcontinent, starting from tentative beginnings in the early nineteenth century as some Indians struggled to critique and reform their own society. The major changes, achieved by over a century and a half of private, public, and legislative initiative, include a move towards ending child marriage and an increase in the average age of marriage, together with an increased element of choice in marital partner by the bride as well as the groom. In tandem with this change has gone greater access to education for girls and young women, from primary to university level, and at some levels of society this has enabled participation in the paid workforce, often in prestigious occupations. As in many societies, rising female educational standards and levels of participation in paid work outside the home have been accompanied by a move to smaller families, partly out of social necessity and partly out of choice, given the greater access of the educated to knowledge about contraception and to health care for mothers and children. Of course not all the lives of women on the subcontinent, or those who have moved away from it in the growing diaspora, have radically changed—far from it. We know only too well the burdens of illiteracy, ill health, and social discrimination which still afflict many women in South Asia. This record does not include those girls who are never born because of foetal selection in favour of boys, or who never survive infancy because of lack of medical care, as shown by the tragic imbalance between men and women in the population even of India as it marches towards becoming an economic powerhouse of the twenty-first century. According to the Indian census of 2001, there were 933 women for every thousand men; and in some regions this figure fell as low as 861. This is a gross departure from the demographic norm; and it does not correlate with poverty but arises from cultural choice.[21] We know too that some of the discriminatory and controlling practices in relation to wives and daughters prevalent in South Asia have been exported in the diaspora. These range from close control of daughters as compared with sons in such matters as clothing, freedom to move around, and choice of friends and marriage partners, to the appalling violence of so-called honour killings, where womenfolk are deemed to have brought dishonour to their families by transgressing norms of social and sexual behaviour.

Although some of the broad trends of social change in women's lives are clearly visible both to the casual eye of any observer of life on the subcontinent and through scholarly reading of available public statistics, we know far less about just how these changes happen in individual families. What is the timing of change, and who is the main driver behind them in terms of family decision making? Is there a key generation in these interlocking changes, and to what extent do official policies and government provisions make a difference to family calculations? It is to try to get at answers to these sorts of questions, I suggest the technique of making a family tree of three or at most four generations and then asking the same questions about the women in each generation. People in Britain or the United States can rarely find the answers to such questions beyond their great-grandparents' generation, though in the case of South Asian families this can be done because early marriage made the generations relatively "short" by comparison with European or American families of the same period. The sorts of questions I have in mind include the standard of education women reached in each generation, whether women married and if so the age of marriage (and if at all possible how the marriage was made, whether by arrangement or some form of individual choice), the numbers of children and their sex, and whether women engaged in outside paid work.

It is possible to track intergenerational change in the lives of a few very public families. For example, in the Nehru family we can trace some of these trends. Nehru's mother was certainly literate in Hindi because he wrote to her in Hindi while he was away in England for his education, though interestingly he wrote to his father in English. In the next generation his two sisters, born around the turn of the twentieth century, were privately educated to a considerable standard. Both published in English, and the older sister became an ambassador. Nehru's daughter, Indira, in turn, born in 1918, went to school at various places in India, then to an English girls' boarding school and thence to Somerville College, Oxford. She of course, after the death of her husband, became her father's hostess and later India's first woman Prime Minister. Nehru's own marriage was arranged by his parents, despite his anxieties about this traditional way of doing things. He hoped at least for someone he knew rather than a total stranger, and for someone with whom there was some degree of mutual understanding.[22] In the end the bride whom his parents chose for him, Kamla, came from his own Kashmiri Brahmin community. However, she came from her own home in Delhi to live with relatives in the Nehru hometown of Allahabad, so that she could get to know her future husband, and also improve her education under the British governess of the two Nehru daughters. She was seventeen when the marriage took place, nearly a decade younger than her groom. This had been a carefully managed departure from more conservative arrangements by the older Nehru generation. Jawaharlal himself had little choice when it came to his own daughter's marriage; and he found himself acquiescing in his daughter's own choice of a husband from a different caste and community, though he knew very little about the man in question and was deeply anxious about the matter. By this time his wife was dead and he was himself in prison as a nationalist leader; and he urged Indira to go to talk to her close relatives and also to Gandhi about it before committing herself.[23] Indira married the man she had chosen for herself, flying in the face of convention, in the year she was twenty-five. We cannot track the marital patterns among the Nehru women any further as Indira herself only had sons. The Nehrus were a most exceptional family with their wide-ranging and often international connections and experiences. Moreover, politics became a family occupation from the 1920s, as the family was swept up into Gandhi's movement against the British. So unpaid public work outside the home in the cause of nationalism became the norm for the women of the family in Jawaharlal's generation, and even his mother went out on the streets to picket foreign cloth shops. Nehru was himself surprised and proud of his wife's newfound interest in the education of women and her influence on that issue—as when one of the women she had talked to in a group in Hyderabad began behaving strangely and failing to be submissive, according to her husband![24] Of course his daughter went from being his political hostess and companion when he, as a widower, became Prime Minister, to being herself Prime Minister of India in 1966.[25] Her elevation to this highest political office obviously owed much to her family connections and experience; but by the second half of the twentieth century elite educated women of her generation were rising high in many professions.

To investigate the viability of doing this type of family life history in more ordinary and less public families I enlisted the help of two of my women Indian doctoral students, both high flyers academically, in that they have achieved this standard at an international university. Both are in their mid- to later twenties, having been born in 1982 and 1981. I use their family life histories with their permission. Megha is from Delhi, was educated wholly in India, and was a Rhodes scholar, coming out of one of Delhi's most prestigious colleges. Sumita was born in the UK to a Bengali family, and both her parents were born in Calcutta. She was educated in England, doing her first degree at Durham University. I should add that neither of them had thought of using their own families as sources of evidence in this way, though both of them had done a master's course with me on social change in modern South Asia! However, they both found the experience of constructing their family trees exciting and illuminating. I owe them both a great debt of gratitude in cooperating in this trial venture. What do their families' life histories stretching back four generation to the last two decades of the nineteenth century tell us about women's experience?

In the first place each young woman is one of two siblings, having a slightly older brother. This is a tiny family compared with the family size of previous generations. Sumita's mother was also one of two siblings, but her father was one of a family of five. Her paternal grandfather was one of eight siblings; while her maternal grandfather was one of a family of seven children. In Megha's case her father was one of three children, while her mother was one of seven. Neither of my students is married. Their mothers both married at a similar age, near the age my students now are—Megha's at twenty-five, and Sumita's (by this time in England) at twenty-seven. But the experience of the older female generation was rather different. Megha's maternal grandmother married at twenty-one in 1938, but Sumita's maternal grandmother married at fourteen (in 1943) and her paternal grandmother married at fifteen (in 1932). These two families in microcosm tell us much about the broader social trends in family size and the age of marriage in the twentieth century.

When we turn to educational standards we need to remember that neither of my young informants comes from a poor family. Poverty is still of course a barrier to education for many millions of Indian girls and young women. Both of these families had status and means by the end of the nineteenth century, from government service, business, or land. However, there are interesting variations in the standard of education received by their womenfolk. Megha's Punjabi-Delhi family has two quite different trends. On her father's side her aunts were educated to B.A. standard, then immediately married, while her father went on to do his M.A. She thinks her grandmother on that side who had only an elementary education was behind the discrimination against her daughters. However, on her mother's side, there was a strong and long tradition of fostering female education which went right back to the great-grandfather born in the 1880s and to his wife. Both the great-grandfather and his son married women who had received some education within their own natal families either at elementary school or from a home tutor, and were determined that their female children should be well educated. In the generation immediately above Megha, four of the children were girls, her aunts, and all received a college education, three of them to M.A. standard, equal to those their brothers achieved. All four of them were the first women of their village (now in Haryana) to attend university in the nearby city of Rohtak and that set something of a village precedent. Sumita's Bengali family experience again has two distinct patterns. Her mother gained a B. Sc. and M. Sc. in London, having migrated to England as a small child. She became a schoolteacher. Her mother in turn had only been educated until her marriage at the age of fourteen; she had to learn English when she settled in England in her twenties. Sumita's father had two younger sisters born in 1945 and 1947. Both gained their Ph.D.s from Calcutta, but neither married. This very high standard of female education had an interesting history. Their mother had home schooling and became literate in Bengali, but she was married at fifteen. Thereafter her husband provided her with an English tutor so she could learn to speak English and talk with his English colleagues and accompany him on social occasions where English would be spoken. She was, according to Sumita, utterly determined that her own daughters would be very well educated and able to fend for themselves in later life, as she had experienced being the daughter of a widow who had had to return to live with her brother. In both families, therefore, it seems that those of the generation born around the end of the First World War, and perhaps the women in particular, were of critical significance in setting the pattern that would be followed by succeeding generations in respect to girls' education and to assumptions about the life expectations of women members of the family. This is of course a tiny example, but it is suggestive of how a larger project in the life history of families can indicate when key social changes occurred, and give a voice to women who would otherwise go unheard by the historian.[26]

I would also like to suggest that this technique of establishing the longitudinal life history of quite ordinary families in this way may also help us to understand the experience of those who migrated out of the subcontinent, particularly those who chose to leave from the 1950s, rather than those who were effectively driven out by necessity in the nineteenth century to become indentured labourers in British colonies where labour was badly needed after the abolition of slavery. For the descendants of such migrants it is probably impossible to get back beyond about 1900 by this means, given the great and traumatic rupture in their lives which indenture overseas constituted, and the fact that the vast majority chose to stay in their new homes once they were free men and women. Many had left in circumstances of dire poverty and had nothing to return to, others had lost touch with whatever relatives they once had, and others were ashamed that their lives and relationships abroad would dishonour their families on the subcontinent.[27] However, for the families of those who migrated from the 1950s there is a real possibility of capturing the experiences of the generation who moved and of several generations subsequently. South Asian outmigration was one of the largest movements of people in the nineteenth and twentieth centuries, generating the contemporary worldwide South Asian diaspora.[28] But again, as in the lives of some of the women we have studied, these were people who rarely generated their own accounts of their decision to move, and their subsequent life experiences in the new homeland, though the Internet is enabling some to contribute their own small piece to the historical mosaic of migration. There is a British website, "Moving Here," which is dedicated to two hundred years of migration into Britain, and it encourages such personal contributions as well as hosting professional pieces of exposition as historical contextualization.[29]

By contrast with the comparative paucity of private information on migrants and their descendants there has been a considerable amount of public collection of information and record making. This is because so often migrants have been perceived as "problem people," politically and socially. In Britain at least records are available of many aspects of migrant lives: numbers of arrivals and timing, housing, health, schooling, and levels of unemployment. The requirements of equal opportunities legislation since the 1970s means that ethnic monitoring occurs at national and local levels, and even within institutions like my own Oxford University, where we monitor the number of ethnic applicants, those who succeed and fail, their educational scores, and compare them with other ethnic groups. As a result of this plethora of public knowledge the broad trends in migration and the experience of migrants into Britain are well known. Although there had been some Indians living in Britain in the nineteenth century,[30] the main flows into Britain happened from the 1950s, soon after the independence of the subcontinent from Britain. The largest numbers of migrants were Indians, followed in numerical terms by Pakistanis and a much smaller group of Bangladeshis. The numbers of Indians were swelled in the early 1970s by those who came from India via East Africa, where many had made their home for several generations but were expelled by the drive for Africanization of key jobs and the economy. It is clear that those of Indian origin have tended to do well in Britain, first in comparatively menial jobs or as self-employed people, but within a generation or two as high-flying professionals and businesspeople. In broad terms those from Pakistan and Bangladesh have done less well, having come with fewer resources in the first place, including lower standards of education, but failing thereafter to move out from this pattern of relative deprivation. Key to the history of these differing trajectories has been the fact that most of those from Pakistan and Bangladesh are Muslim, while the large numbers of Hindus and Sikhs among the Indians is significant. Hindus and Sikhs do not retain the close cousin marital bonds that Muslims do with their ancestral homelands, and the material and social investment in their former homes that this requires. Moreover, they encourage their girls to take advantage of the provision of education in Britain, free at least to the end of secondary school and relatively inexpensive at college level, and to take up the employment opportunities this in turn offers. (At the end of the twentieth century over half of the Indian women aged sixteen and over were employed, compared with 27 percent for Pakistanis and 22 percent for Bangladeshi women.)[31] The fact that the women of Indian families coming from East Africa had high standards of education and traditions of economic participation there reinforced this trend within the Indian community as a whole in Britain.

Historians studying the experience of South Asian migration could deepen our understanding of some of these trends by examining individual diaspora family trajectories in much the same way as I have already outlined for the study of women's experience in South Asia. Significantly, while I was thinking about this work it was announced in Britain that there would be a longitudinal study of the health of a sample of diaspora families to enable the state to understand the particular medical problems of South Asian Britons. So historians are clearly not alone in thinking that this is an important strategy for "doing history." In particular this technique of doing family history would help us to understand the decision to migrate, changing attitudes to education for boys and girls, levels of educational achievement across generations, and subsequent patterns of employment and social mobility. Comparison of the size of families with migrant origins will also indicate the usual correlation with female education and paid work, just as it does on the subcontinent. In broad terms we know that Indian families in Britain tend to be smaller already than those of their ancestors and those of the two other South Asian groups in Britain among whom women's educational levels were or are lower.[32] A further aspect of South Asian migration to Britain has been what is called "chain migration"—people following their relatives and neighbours from the same village and area in "chains" when word got back to South Asia of what could be achieved in Britain. The website "Moving Here" tells of one Pakistani family from Mirpur of which 135 family members have settled in Britain. Individual family history could also uncover other such chains of migrating relatives.

Let us examine this strategy now, just in relation to the decision to move overseas to Britain. The broad picture of migrants' origins suggests that they tended to come from areas of South Asia where there were already patterns of movement and consequent opening of horizons and willingness to encounter change. Bangladeshis and those from parts of Pakistani Kashmir came from areas where there were traditions of riverine trade and then male employment in British ships as sailors and stokers. This seems to have established patterns of movement for later generations. Sylhet in Bangladesh, for example, has provided the vast majority of so-called Indian restaurateurs in Britain, while Mirpur in Pakistan was the ancestral home of many Pakistani migrants. It has been estimated that 90 percent of Pakistanis now living in Bradford and Birmingham originated from that one district. Gujaratis often came to the UK via East Africa, where their ancestors had moved in the early twentieth century across the Arabian Sea, for trade or in the service of the expanding British Empire. Many Punjabis, another large group of migrants, from both sides of the India-Pakistan border, had already been displaced at par-

tition in 1947 and moved on again abroad within a generation. Another pattern of prior movement was of course travel as a student,
which seems to have prepared and predisposed people for later permanent moves abroad.

If we take my student, Sumita, we shall find this student pattern
in her family experience on both the maternal and paternal sides. Her
father came to London as a student in 1969 and stayed on. He married
a woman who had come to England as a child when the family joined
their father, who had also come to England as a student, to study law,
and stayed on. It is also significant that Sumita's paternal grandfather
had himself moved—from his village to Calcutta, and his father in
turn had worked for the railways, that great institution that brought
physical movement to the mass of the South Asian population in the
later nineteenth century. I have three academic colleagues in Oxford of
Indian ethnic origin, two from Bengal and one from Mauritius, which
means of course that his ancestors had already moved from the subcontinent. For all three the student experience in Britain was the pre-
cursor to employment in Britain, either immediately or after a period
of time, and then permanent settlement. An English woman colleague
of mine at London University is married to an academic of South
Asian origin. His family history shows in considerable detail the patterns of movement generated both by the student experience but also
by the upheavals of partition. His family of Muslims from the United
Provinces in northern India had moved into the city and into the professions by the early twentieth century, as had Sumita's paternal grandfather. His father went to Britain to study engineering at London University in 1938 and eventually joined the colonial irrigation service in
Sindh, where he found himself on the Pakistani side of the new border in 1947. His extended family soon joined him by various means,
mercifully being spared the horrors that engulfed so many of the refu-
gees in both directions. Although this generation stayed in Pakistan,
many of the family's younger generation were sent abroad for education, including the son who married my colleague. (Interestingly his
four brothers were educated outside Pakistan but not their one sister.)

It is this generation that has produced many international migrants—to Britain, the Gulf, America, and Canada. As one more example of a family's life history that indicates the power of an established pattern of movement, and also the political changes that might force mobile families to move yet again, let me offer the experience of a distinguished alumnus of my own college, now a prominent lawyer in London. He was born in Tanganyika, as it was then, to a Gujarati Brahmin family that had moved to Africa in the 1940s. In 1968 the family moved with their small son, aged four, and his older siblings to settle permanently in London, out of reach of the forces of African nationalism which had made their African home an unstable base for a family.

Family lives are clearly the building blocks of much larger trends in social history. Broad trends in demographic change, particularly large-scale migration, rest on the decisions of individual families and kin groups as they weigh up opportunities and dangers, often in the light of prior familial and kin experience of different kinds of movement. In the same way significant social trends, such as those relating to the experience of women in India, are built by the cumulative responses of individuals and their families to their past and present experiences, to new opportunities and to new ideas and aspirations. The experiences of particular families as they make key decisions are an important source for historians, and often they allow us to know more about the lives of people who rarely enter the public record. As historians we may have to learn new techniques to access such evidence, but it will enrich our historical understanding and open new windows onto the relatively recent past.

CHAPTER 3

Individual Lives
and Their Public World

In the first two chapters I expanded the more usual understanding of "life history," beyond the life of an individual, to include the life of key institutions and of families, as ways of doing history. I argued that engaging with these different sorts of "lives" might open new windows on to the recent South Asian past, though of course the technique could also illuminate the history of other places and times. Now I turn to the lives of individuals, particularly those accepted as being notable and historically significant, but in a rather different way from a biographer whose aim is to tell a life story rather than use a particular life to understand a wider historical setting or set of issues. How might the historian of South Asia use such life histories? Here I focus on individuals and their public world, and in chapter 4 I shall turn to individuals and their inner worlds, particularly their moral and intellectual struggles and debates with themselves and their circles of friends and colleagues. The two topics are obviously intertwined; but it is a division that is convenient for our analytical purposes.

At the outset I underline that I am not a biographer, even though I have written major life histories of Mahatma Gandhi and Jawaharlal Nehru.[1] A biographer conventionally tries to piece together a whole life in all its dimensions in considerable detail, because the analytical focus is the individual and the unfolding of his or her life. You will not find in my works many things that a biographer might include—for example, a detailed account of family relations and friendships, except where these impinge on a broader historical analysis. To take one example, people often and irritatingly ask me about Nehru's relationship with Edwina Mountbatten, wife of the last British Viceroy. For me the exact physical nature of their friendship is far less important, and indeed impossible to prove, compared with her significance over many years as a sounding board for his hopes and fears, when he had few within India he felt he could trust implicitly. Looked at this way their long-term friendship, often conducted by airmail letters, is a window into the Prime Minister's isolated position as well as his key concerns. Using an individual's life can prove deeply rewarding as a way into historical analysis of important trends or crucial phases of history, as I shall argue. It also addresses two concerns that I noted at the outset of this work. It is a way of communicating serious history to a larger and historically hungry public. I have been amazed and gratified by the great variety of people who have read my two life histories of Gandhi and Nehru, and am convinced of the importance of reaching beyond academia to offer serious historical analysis through this genre.

However, life histories of individuals are also an important point of access to new historical sources. We stand at a point in time in relation to the recent history of South Asia when new written sources are still being found and opened to research—particularly the private papers and records of people involved in politics and public life. It is a fascinating question why these materials were kept by those who accumulated them, as authors or recipients, for most people throw away much of their personal paperwork once it is no longer important on a daily personal or business basis. You have to value a written record greatly to preserve it over decades or longer. It may be personally significant in the case of a love affair, a close friendship, or a major life event, or as an important reflection of personal and public achievement or controversy. Some people of course hang on to personal papers through sheer inertia. Quite recently I met an eminent British scientist who had worked briefly in India as a young army doctor in the closing years of the Second World War. When I asked him if he had kept any material from his India days, he went delving in his attic and brought to the history faculty in Oxford old shopping bags of miscellaneous papers, ranging from wedding invitations to letters home and formal reports he had made of his army activities. It was a historian's treasure trove just because it was the accumulated detritus of an ordinary life. The Indian public activists whose papers are now being collected, catalogued, and made available to scholars, were by contrast well aware that they were living at a critical time and were actually "making history." Keeping their papers was part of the business of creating a new nation-state, as well as staking their own claims to have played a role in that creation. Giving the new India its proper history was also uppermost in the minds of those who have provided archival space for such collections, particularly the Nehru Memorial Library in New Delhi.

If we take the two individuals whose lives I have been most concerned with, the magnitude and variety of their papers is astounding. Gandhi's published *Collected Works* now run to over ninety volumes and include letters, speeches, newspaper articles, and lengthier occasional works, as well as scrawled notes on the back of odd papers written on his famous day of silence once a week. Nehru's papers include similar personal and political material, and of course much more official paperwork dating from his decade and a half as Prime Minister, including letters written to him or copies of other correspondence sent to him. He would keep even seemingly insignificant notes—such as his irate demand for wastepaper baskets in the Ministry of External Affairs as he felt it was so dirty, or his request for records of his cabinet colleagues' consumption of electricity when

India was enduring a power crisis and he could see their lights burning from his home. I calculated on one research visit using these papers that if I were to read everything he had retained as Prime Minister I would probably have to work solidly for eight years. Many of those who played a prominent role in the history of India and particularly of India's struggle for independence also self-consciously offered their lives for public consumption through the genre of autobiography—as we saw in the last chapter. Some of course were only partial, written during rare interludes of leisure provided by ill health or by prison sentences. Gandhi never progressed beyond 1920, when he was just on the threshold of the most significant phase of his career in India. Nehru's autobiography concluded when he was forty-five, in prison in 1935. He admitted to feeling at times "a sense of age and weariness";[2] but it would be another decade before he stood on the threshold of what many would argue were his most important years. The intentions of those who wrote autobiographies were manifold, some overt and some barely articulated—they were variously didactic, self-justifying, or part of a quest for selfhood and self-understanding as well as a search for Indian-ness in a fast-changing world. If a historian is aware of the complex nature of such documents, these too can be important sources for engaging with individual life history.[3] It is significant that in the twenty-first century former Untouchables, those at the base of Hindu society, are now also beginning to use the genre of autobiography as a powerful political statement of their newly reconstructed identity as Dalits.[4]

Let me turn now to the lives of Gandhi and Nehru to investigate how their lives open windows into the public world they inhabited. The broad outline of their two lives is well known. Both were born as subjects of Queen Victoria. Gandhi, born in 1869 and the older by twenty years, came from Gujarat in western India, where his father worked for several princely states. On his father's untimely death he was sent to England to study law in the hope that he would become the cornerstone of his family's prosperity. Instead he failed to make a career in law in India and went to South Africa on a year's legal contract. He stayed for twenty years. On his return to India in 1915 he was a mature public figure, skilled in political activism on behalf of Indians facing discrimination in South Africa. In particular he had honed a method of direct but nonviolent resistance to wrongs of many kinds, which he called *satyagraha,* or truth force, to distinguish it from passive resistance. From 1920 he was a major figure in the politics of Indian nationalism, and the leader of several India-wide movements of civil resistance against the British. He was assassinated in 1948. Nehru came from a far wealthier family; we looked briefly into his family home in the previous chapter. He was educated in England, at Harrow, Cambridge, and the Inns of Court, and returned to India to join his father in his legal practice. He was swept up into the politics of nationalism under the aegis of Gandhi and remained in politics all his life. He was India's first Prime Minister from 1947, remaining in office until his death in 1964, having quite literally worn himself out in the service of his country. A closer look at these remarkable lives allows the historian to engage with several key analytical themes in modern India's history—particularly the nature of the politics of nationalism, the painful and often contested emergence of a sense of nationhood, the creation of a modern nation-state, and the different types of leadership within a complex political system. Given that both men became essentially all-India leaders rather than emerging through and being rooted in the politics of localities and regions, their lives also particularly illuminate the potential and problems of being an all-India leader, and by extension the nature of the Indian political system that was emerging in these decades, and the many problems of integrating different levels of politics into a national political system. It is the issues relating particularly to the nature of all-India leadership on which I now wish to focus, using them as a case study in the usefulness of individual life history.

We must start with the particular entry points into national political life of these two men; for they are most revealing and quite unlike the paths into national politics trodden by most of their contemporaries. Of course both had received education in English, which gave them the common language to communicate with their compatriots across the subcontinent. Both also had the sort of higher education abroad that gave them political credence in India and, more important, the perspective which made them visualise India as a whole and envisage its problems in the global terms of worldwide imperialism. It is significant that Gandhi wrote his seminal text on Indian home rule, *Hind Swaraj,* while outside India—in 1909 on a boat between Britain and South Africa.[5] However, as he prepared to return to India permanently he did not envisage entering politics but planned on a life of social work and of personal piety. Both men were in a very real sense outsiders to India's political world. Gandhi had grown up in a political backwater on the subcontinent hardly touched by modern politics; he spent twenty years away from India, in South Africa; and his increasingly simple and religious lifestyle—which many saw as profoundly idiosyncratic if not downright odd—was fashioned by personal preoccupations with the search for truth which had come to dominate his life during the first decade of the twentieth century.[6] Nehru was also somewhat remote from the rough and tumble of Indian politics because of his family expectations and his own inclinations. Motilal Nehru, who had made such a successful career in law, without the benefit of an English legal training, had even higher ambitions for his beloved only son. At first he hoped his son would go into the most prestigious of careers: the ICS, career home to the many Balliol men we encountered earlier in this volume. When it became clear that the younger Nehru would not obtain high enough results at Cambridge to contemplate this, the father's sights turned to law and the hope that his son would join and then carry on his own legal practice in Allahabad. Jawaharlal in turn was bored by the law and thoroughly disillusioned by the armchair politics of his father's associates and contemporaries. For a political career in the early twentieth century in India was not a full-time occupation, but more like an interest carried on alongside a profession such as law or teaching. It often involved collaborating with the imperial rulers by working in the emerging political institutions of consultation which the British had gradually been constructing at the local, provincial, and national level. It might also mean participating in local gatherings to address matters of local concern, or attending the annual meetings of the recently formed Indian National Congress, which was a sounding board for political opinion but not a well-organised party that could work the year round and offer a serious full-time career. By contrast the younger Nehru hankered for a more aggressive politics of nationalism against the British, but there seemed little scope for this, and his ideas were beginning to cause tensions with his father.[7]

The dramatic change in the Indian political scene which gave these two outsiders the opportunity to enter politics was caused by the First World War. Under its influence, and given the thousands of Indian soldiers who served the British cause, fighting as far away as the Western front in France, the British moved to accommodate rising political demand with the 1917 declaration that their goal for India was "responsible government." There followed a period of consultation and then the reconstruction of the provincial and central legislatures, through the so-called Montagu-Chelmsford Reforms of 1919, named after the Secretary of State for India and the Viceroy of the day. These were designed to open the door to real power for Indian politicians who could win the votes of an enlarged but still quite small electorate. It seemed to the British rulers that this expanded political system would attract just the range of allies the British desired—educated local men who had their fingers on the pulse of local problems and could rely on local support.[8] However, their well-laid plans were blown out of the water by two interlocking crises: the Muslim concern for the future of the Khalifah, the Sultan of Turkey, whose fate seemed desperate after his defeat; and the revulsion amongst almost all Indians who heard of the shocking massacre of nearly 350 unarmed people at Amritsar in 1919 on the orders of a British general. (In chapter 2 we saw how the Balliol-educated Lieutenant-Governor of Punjab, the province in which Amritsar was located, Sir Michael O'Dwyer, paid for this incident with his life well after retirement. Whether the assassin intended him as the victim, or whether he mistook him for the army officer who ordered the shooting, General Reginald Dyer, is unclear.) On the wave of political feeling generated by these two crises, Gandhi emerged most unexpectedly as the dominant figure in the Indian National Congress in 1920, successfully arguing for a campaign of noncooperation with the British and their institutions, including their schools, colleges, and their recently reformed legislatures. For him it was the perfect opportunity to try out in India on a large scale the type of moral resistance and renewal he believed had been so successful in South Africa, *satyagraha,* or truth force. For the many who rather surprisingly agreed to withdraw their cooperation with the rulers, it offered a new and potentially influential way of attempting to put pressure on the British.[9] For his part, the young Nehru, blasé and disillusioned, was electrified by this new force in politics and determined to join Gandhi, despite Motilal's initial hesitations. As Jawaharlal later wrote, "Many of us who worked for the Congress programme lived in a kind of intoxication during the year 1921. We were full of excitement and optimism and a buoyant enthusiasm. We sensed the happiness of a person crusading for a cause. . . . Above all, we had a sense of freedom and a pride in that freedom. The old feeling of oppression and frustration was completely gone."[10] It was as Gandhi's protégé that he entered politics, as an ardent player in an all-India protest movement. He subsequently became one of the most significant of the younger generation in the party and in the unfolding politics of nationalism.

The particular circumstances of the entry of Gandhi and Nehru into Indian politics tell the historian much about the public and political world they encountered. Here was a political system in flux, institutionally and ideologically. On the one hand the British were constructing for their own ends a pan-Indian system of elective institutions that offered real power at provincial and all-India levels to Indian politicians who chose to cooperate with them, and could base their claim to political influence and place by making connections with the greater numbers of voters enfranchised under the new system. As I think the imperial rulers well understood, they were constructing institutions that would help to weld an integrative political system that was pan-Indian in horizontal terms but also integrated Indian politics in a vertical direction, by linking elite politicians to at least some of the political concerns and modalities that thrived in the localities. By so doing they hoped to tame and train aspiring political activists, and channel their energies away from the politics of nationalist opposition to imperial rule into the constructive work that the new legislatures enabled, in such areas as health, education, and economic development. It was an extension of a policy that they had developed at the local level in the 1880s when they began to devolve power over local government to Indians. As a senior member of the Government of India had observed then, "We shall not subvert the British empire by allowing the Bengali Baboo to discuss his own schools and drains. Rather shall we afford him a safety-valve if we can turn his attention to such innocuous subjects."[11] After 1919 Indian politicians had to operate in a changing world: they had to learn to work new institutions, and to elicit support from new kinds of local people. But this was also just at the time when external events made them doubt both the worth of the new system and the intentions of their rulers. This unique juncture of events provided opportunities for many different kinds and levels of political activity in India. There were increasingly powerful roles for those who remained in their provinces, satisfying their electors, and becoming significant local players as members of the provincial legislatures by deploying the new resources and decision-making power available through them. Many of them also became at least nominal members of their local branch of Congress, using its repute and name, and strengthening their local position with wider alliances across the country. A good example of this sort of political figure was G. B. Pant, a small-town lawyer from the United Provinces who rose via work in the UP legislatures and Congress to become Chief Minister of UP in 1937–39 and again after independence.[12] But for every Pant there were thousands more provincial political operators who increasingly recognised the importance of the new provincial political arena opening up to them, the local leverage to be had as a provincial member of the legislative assembly, and at times the potential of the Congress organisation as a mechanism for forwarding their local careers. However, for most of the 1920s and 1930s their sights were set primarily on their provinces, and national politics and organisations were rarely of significance to them. It was not surprising that when Gandhi and Nehru enquired into the "health" of the Congress organisation in 1929 when a renewal of civil disobedience seemed likely, and made a functioning local organisation vital, they found that often the provincial or local Congress was little more than a nameplate on a lawyer's door.[13]

There were fewer but nonetheless important roles for people who were mainly all-India players, men who were not rooted in the provincial and local power structures but who were able to consolidate Congress policies across the country and to help their compatriots deal with their rulers by speaking, or at least claiming to speak, for the country at large. However, it proved far more difficult to construct a political career as an all-India politician working in the imperial legislature, and trying to consolidate the policies of provincial groups of legislators, than to build up a local position as a member of the provincial legislature with access to influence and patronage, as Motilal Nehru discovered in the 1920s. The drivers of legislative politics lay mainly in the provinces, and all-India policies and stances, and attempted political groupings, tended to unravel.[14] More rarely occasions might arise that demanded all-India leaders to mastermind campaigns of resistance to the British. When this happened it was particularly important that those who were in a sense the political elite at the national and provincial levels should also be able, through the work of an all-India leadership, to connect not just with each other but to align their campaigns with much more popular and local causes, to give credence to the status they claimed as spokesmen for the nation. So here was another political role, another job opportunity, for an individual or group with integrative vision and skills. Gandhi and Nehru both became essentially all-India politicians, entering politics at this level as we have seen. Neither was really rooted in provincial politics, deriving strength from a place in particular local power structures, and neither made provincial politics his main concern or domain. They were to draw strength and status from the skills they deployed and the roles they performed at an all-India level in the system. So it is to their roles and functions we must now turn, having seen how their remarkable entry into politics can be a window into that system at a crucial juncture in its development.

Gandhi's Indian career was encapsulated almost completely in the phase of growing nationalist demand, and he never embarked on a career within independent India, as Nehru had to, so his all-India role is easier to analyse. This is not the place for a detailed examination of what he did,[15] but I shall tease out some crucial themes to show how we may learn from his life in Indian politics, particularly about the nature of continental leadership. He was first and foremost an ideologue with an enormously wide appeal. He spoke, wrote, and indeed lived the idea of *swaraj,* or self-rule and freedom, in a way that resonated with the educated and uneducated, young and old, men and women. Many came to dispute his vision of a new India, including many Muslims and Untouchables at the base of Hindu society, those who had either a fundamentally Hindu view of India or envisaged a radical socialist revolution, and those who felt he was suggesting that India should revert to a simple village society and throw away the advantages of a modern economy. But for many more Indians he offered the prospect of an India free of colonial rule which touched the hearts and minds of millions and offered the prospect of change in the areas where people longed for a new order. In a time before mass communications he was a genius at reaching larger numbers than any politicians before him. Even those in politics who disagreed with some of the nuances of his ideal of *swaraj* recognised that a nationalist movement would be more powerful and rooted in popular support with him as its leader, and were loath to challenge him. Moreover, he also offered his countrymen a new mode of managing their relationship with the British—*satyagraha.* He had worked to refine this mode of resistance to many types of wrongs, as he saw them, while

in South Africa, and then in local situations back in India, sometimes
against other Indians, in 1917–18. Pan-Indian nonviolent resistance
to aspects of colonial rule made considerable sense to many nation-
alists when they knew that the British essentially determined the rules
of politics and were quite prepared to clamp down on violent protest
and to ignore polite petitioning. But as a regime the raj relied on Indians in many collaborative roles, and if their crucial allies withdrew
their services, then it would be severely weakened. *Satyagraha* had other
benefits. It was so flexible that it could be adapted to suit the local
politics of different regions, encouraging into the ranks of activists
those who had powerful local grievances, and it was hospitable to all
sorts of people who had never participated in politics before. For
example, the boycott of foreign cloth was an aspect of *satyagraha* that
drew in women in their hundreds. Before that campaign virtually no
respectable woman would have been seen on the streets in public
protest; but Gandhi made such public activism not only respectable
but a highly moral way of helping build up a free nation. (Remember
how we saw in chapter 2 that even Jawaharlal's elderly mother went
out to boycott foreign cloth.) Moreover, *satyagraha* was in a real sense
a public spectacle—even public theatre. Large-scale meetings in
spaces once controlled by the British, carefully choreographed dem-
onstrations of peaceful disobedience to colonial laws, such as Gandhi's
famous salt march to the coast to make salt in 1930, the willingness
of many thousands to court prison peacefully—all these were very
public and well-produced challenges to British authority.[16] As such
satyagraha posed novel and taxing problems for the British in how to
respond to this new mode of peaceful opposition. It attracted huge
attention throughout the subcontinent, but also abroad, particularly
in Britain and America, just at a time when the British were very conscious of their own domestic and international critics of imperialism.
How they were to treat Gandhi became deeply political and contentious,[17] and consequently increased Gandhi's "value" to his compatriots in politics.

Another profoundly significant aspect of Gandhi's all-India work
in the Congress party itself was his role as a unifier. He recognised

that it contained people of many different viewpoints, but he was determined wherever possible to unify the organisation in the face of the Indian public and also of the British rulers, to give credence to its claims to speak for the nation. When internal disputes broke out he did his utmost to soothe frayed nerves and battered egos, and reminded his colleagues of their shared goal. Almost always they deferred to him rather than split apart the movement and weaken their status and claims.[18] Sometimes even more publicly he would agree to let some congressmen follow their own path, as in the mid-1920s when he acquiesced in the strategy of using the legislatures in the name of Congress rather than noncooperation, by men such as Motilal Nehru and C. R. Das. Or he would withdraw a strategy he held dear rather than split the Congress. This lay behind his decision to release congressmen from *satyagraha* in 1934 when he knew that so many of them were disillusioned with it and longed to return to the politics of the legislatures.

However, Gandhi's place in Indian political life was ambiguous and his influence uneven over the course of the three decades he spent enmeshed in the campaign for *swaraj*. This is often not recognised by people who know little about India, particularly the younger generation introduced to Gandhi by the immensely popular but somewhat simplistic film of his life which appeared in 1982. But Gandhi's apparent failures and the times when he seemed to have little influence are as instructive to the historian as his times of great popularity and achievement. The times when he retired to his ashram home with no apparent role in politics are as important as windows into the politics of the day as the times when he was clearly the main spokesman of Indian nationalism—as when he achieved a famous pact with the Viceroy in 1931 to end civil disobedience, or when he attended the Round Table Conference in London in 1931. (Incidentally, during this visit he stayed twice for the weekend in Balliol College—another sign of the college's deep links with the subcontinent.)[19]

Some of Gandhi's problems as an all-India leader stemmed from *satyagraha* itself. It proved a profoundly difficult enterprise to direct and control when it was stretched across a whole subcontinent, as

compared with the much smaller movements he had led in South
Africa or back in India in 1917–18. It could either peter out or, more
dangerously, erupt into violence precisely when it drew into its em-
brace local people and movements with their own very different agendas. In such cases Gandhi felt he had to end the movements for both
moral and political reasons. The most dramatic instance was in Feb-
ruary 1922, after a mob had attacked a police station in Chauri Chaura
in UP and killed the Indian policemen inside it.[20] Gandhi as the archi-
tect of pan-Indian nonviolent movements of protest and withdrawal
of cooperation from the raj also found that congressmen were not
permanent converts to *satyagraha,* and did not believe, as he did, that
it was the only seriously moral way of dealing with wrong, in this
case with British rule. For most of them their response to *satyagraha*
was governed by its utility. At certain junctures, as in 1920 or 1930, it
seemed an excellent way of relating to and dealing with the British
while at the same time attracting popular support. But at other times
the lure of work in the new legislatures proved far stronger, in antici-
pation that such collaborative roles within the political system would
give them access to real local power and also build strong links with
local followings. In 1934, for example, when Gandhi recognised this
and withdrew civil disobedience, he likened his colleagues to people
who hankered after *jelabis,* a particularly luscious Indian sweet![21] Again
with extreme reluctance he agreed in the late 1930s that Congress
should fight the elections under the new constitution of 1935 which
gave the provinces autonomy; and further, when Congress was tri-
umphantly successful in those elections, that its members should hold
provincial office. He was a realist, and saw that this was the best way
of keeping Congress together even though it took Congress down
a political path of which he profoundly disapproved. He would have
agreed with Lord Acton about the corrupting influence of power, and
when his colleagues took office he was soon concerned about the ease
with which they seemed to have slipped into the governing role, and
how like their imperial rulers they were becoming, instead of being
the servants of their compatriots. It was evident that his influence in
politics waned whenever there was an attractive prospect of serious

power through collaboration with the regime, and when confrontational politics offered little leverage either over the British or over local issues. Gandhi's influence finally ebbed away from 1945 when it was clear that the British were going soon and *satyagraha* would serve no useful political purpose to politicians active at the national or provincial level. His career had shown the acute problems of exercising political influence and leadership at the all-India level in the context of nationalism, when he believed that a particular style of resistance was moral and constructive, while his colleagues judged it in an entirely different fashion. He retained an all-India role only because of his other activities, such as work for the ending of untouchability, or the furthering of cottage industries and village uplift, which he thought were central to the creation of a truly free India. He also preserved his position and the potential to re-emerge in active politics by working with a group of key allies who took over the specifically political leadership roles at the all-India level when he withdrew to create, as he saw it, *swaraj* from the roots upwards.

Nehru's career had a very different trajectory. He was of comparatively little significance as an all-India leader in his own right until the later 1930s at the earliest, and really not until after the Second World War ended. He came into Congress as Gandhi's protégé, and such power as he did wield was really as a Congress functionary at Gandhi's behest. For his part Gandhi believed he must keep Nehru in play rather than allowing him to slip on to the sidelines of political life as a disgruntled radical, because he believed Nehru could speak to a younger generation and to those of more radical tendencies, and would help to keep them within a united nationalist movement. He also felt that Nehru was a man of huge talents and integrity, which would one day be important for the new nation. Nehru without Gandhi really had no power base, not even in his home province. He did not participate in the provincial or all-India legislatures, and he was often deeply uneasy in his relationships with the other leaders who clustered round Gandhi. He only really came into his own and showed what a communicator he might be during the campaigning for the 1936–37 elections. After his release from prison at the end of the Second World War it was clear that Gandhi had aged and lost much of the leverage he had once had in politics, and he supported Nehru as his heir. Congressmen recognised that Nehru, with this special status, with his own skills as a potential popular democratic party leader, and having the background to deal with the British in the final diplomacy of decolonization, was the person now able to play a number of vital roles for them and their country. He became the Chief Minister in the final interim British government, and then Prime Minister of independent India until his death. He was also at various times President of Congress, and for the whole span of his premiership his own Minister of External Affairs.

Scholars of the postcolonial world have surprisingly paid comparatively little attention to the way men who like Nehru emerged into public life through the politics of nationalism, then in a very real sense had to retrain themselves to become democratic leaders and also administrators. Governing is a very different process from constructing and leading a nationalist movement, as is leading a party in power compared with a protest movement with a common enemy. Nehru knew the Congress party from the inside, having been at various times its President or one of its Secretaries, often at Gandhi's behest. So the business of managing the Congress once it became the party of power was not totally new to him. But he had never been a minister in any of the provincial governments of the 1920s or 1930s, because he had never stood for election. Indeed, his only experience of "government" was some months as chairman of the municipal board of his hometown, Allahabad, in the early 1920s. Rather to his own surprise he found that he enjoyed this. Initially anxious about wandering "in the shady alleys and lands of constitutional activity," as he put it, he soon discovered that even at that lowly level of governance it was possible to make a difference to people's lives.[22] What can his attempts to retrain himself to perform his new roles after 1947, and his subsequent experiences tell the historian? Can they be for us windows particularly on the Indian political system?

One of Nehru's most urgent problems after independence was managing the Congress and turning it into a democratic party capable

of winning elections and carrying through policies while in government, in contrast to its earlier role as a movement of protest. Moreover, he had to ensure that this now dominant and inclusive party,
holding together many shades of opinion and regional groupings,
did not overwhelm the processes of democratic government by its
members and their clients subverting the administration. At first he
tried to dominate the party, even threatening to resign from politics if
congressmen did not accept his priorities—but knowing well that
few would have risked such an eventuality. Later he delegated the role
of president to other people, but still maintained a deep interest in its
membership and its behaviour at the level of the new states (built on
the old provinces) as well as at the all-India level. His real problem
was that he wanted Congress to be a crucial mechanism for forwarding his national policies of nation building: building a new economy,
dealing with poverty, reforming some of the major social problems
identified during the nationalist struggle, and constructing a sense of
inclusive nationalism, which would give a secure and valued place for
India's minorities in the new world of freedom. Instead it was what
became known by analysts as an "umbrella party." Its very success in
winning elections and becoming the dominant party in the country
rested on incorporating into itself a huge variety of opinions, and
also in each region and locality reflecting the dominant power structures and drawing strength from them. People of all sorts found their
way into the party as they recognised that it was the key career structure for anyone who wanted to be a successful politician. These trends
had started in the late 1930s when Congress briefly formed provincial
governments across much of India, but they accelerated after Congress effectively inherited the raj in 1947.[23] This made it less and less
the sort of party that could perform the role Nehru hoped from it.
He became deeply frustrated—at its tendency to factional disputes in
the states as different groups struggled for power within it, and at his
inability to insist that local Congress parties support his national
policies. Discriminatory treatment of Muslims in his home state of
Uttar Pradesh, and persecution of Christians in Madhya Pradesh were
cases in point, where the local Congress parties and governments

went their own way despite prime ministerial protestations. His un-
characteristically undemocratic dismissal in 1959 of the first elected
Communist government in a state, in Kerala, was again forced on him
by the state Congress party and its eagerness to retain power and to
protect the position of its supporters in local life. The stress of this
crisis actually made Nehru ill, and he had to have a holiday in the hills
to recover. Managing the party was clearly far more difficult now that
the common enemy, the British, had been removed, as had Gandhi's
emollient presence. Moreover the stakes in local politics were now
very high—serious power to mould public life, and to reinforce or
undermine existing power structures and vested interests. It was little
wonder that local congressmen had their own political agendas that
might not coincide with the lofty priorities of a government in Delhi.
Nehru never resolved the problem of his relationship with the party,
often resorting to hectoring criticism of it as a sign of his dislike of
this aspect of his work, and perhaps his inability to recognise the naturally evolving nature of democratic politics on a subcontinent.

Nehru as Prime Minister had really no role models. He knew
something about the way Britain's political system functioned but
not in any detail. (It is rather touching that later when an academic
book was published on the role of the prime minister he bought it for
his personal library.) So he forged his own role and style. He clearly
felt that he had the right and duty to lead the nation by setting out
clear reformist and constructive policies and pushing them through,
exhorting his colleagues in government as well as the country at large.[24]
It would be possible, if not entirely accurate, to describe his style as a
combination of the didactic Gandhi and an imperial viceroy. Mountbatten told him that not even Churchill would have treated his colleagues in the high-handed way Nehru did. More dangerously, Nehru
tried to do far too much. He did not just combine the roles of Prime
Minister and Minister for External Affairs. He seemed not to know
how to delegate, and in these roles attempted to intervene in the most
minute details of government. (Remember the wastepaper basket
and electricity bills I mentioned earlier?) Not only did he wear himself

out, he also failed to understand when things were going seriously wrong or to tackle them. Moreover, when he was abroad on numerous foreign visits or when his health began to fail at the end, the business of government at the centre tended to slow down if not grind to a halt. Nehru's punishing workload and his personal frustrations show the problems of trying to govern a free India democratically. Just as historians have put together a picture of an imperial raj stretching its sway across the subcontinent with changing political institutions and judicious attraction of key allies, so Nehru's tenure of the highest office in Delhi shows us some of the acute problems of replacing that raj with a democratic government. How can a government in Delhi relate to its party base? Who are the centre's reliable allies and collaborators in a federal structure that gives considerable power to the states, to the point of frustrating the centre's policies? And how does Delhi relate to the great variety of state politics and power structures?

The public life histories of Gandhi and Nehru were so different, yet both were central to the making of modern India. Their achievements and the power they were able to wield at the all-India level, as well as their failings and frustrations, open windows on to some of the great themes and issues in India's history. Through their lives we can study the contentious business of creating national identity and a nationalist movement, and of nation building after the end of empire. We can also examine through their lives the structures of politics and governance, and in particular look at the interconnections between different levels of political organisations, institutions, and activity. Gandhi and Nehru show us the potential roles of an all-India leader, but also the constraints within which such people have to operate because of the size of India and its diversity. These issues are still with us more than forty years after Nehru's death and are still urgent, as India in the twenty-first century tries to reconstruct itself, just as Gandhi and Nehru had tried to recreate it in their generations.

CHAPTER 4

Individual Lives and
Their Inner World

The third and fourth chapters of this exploration into "life histories" are concerned with the lives of prominent individual Indians,
particularly Mahatma Gandhi and Jawaharlal Nehru, to see how this
genre may be a creative way of doing history rather distinct from the
art form of biography. In chapter 3 we examined how their life experiences in Indian politics can open a window for historians into
that public and political world, and gave us access to, and evidence of,
some key issues in the analysis of Indian politics which are still important today. There were hints, however, of inner motivations and
struggles. It is to their inner world I wish to turn now. I hope to show
how the lives of these two very different men demonstrate and illuminate some of the great problems and debates they and many of their
compatriots faced, at a time when India was changing in many ways
at a faster rate and more radically than in the lives of their ancestors.

Both Gandhi and Nehru generated considerable evidence of their inner concerns and struggles. Both were very self-aware, highly articulate, and skilled writers, using vernacular languages and English. Nehru's natural choice for the written word was English and his language was elegant and persuasive. Gandhi's education had been less privileged than Nehru's, and he did not feel at ease in English until he was forced into fluency by his studies in London. He learned to write powerfully in English as well as his native Gujarati, though many of his longer pieces were translated and polished by his devoted secretary, Mahadev Desai. Both Gandhi and Nehru worked out their self-questioning in a range of literature designed for public consumption. Gandhi, as we have seen, wrote a partial autobiography in the 1920s. His other main works included his key 1909 exposition of true freedom for India, *Hind Swaraj,* a history of his *satyagraha* movement in South Africa, and numerous other pamphlets on immediate and urgent problems as they arose—for example, on the problem of treating as untouchable those at the base of Hindu society, and the nature of his so-called Constructive Programme, which he felt was the foundation of true self-rule. Nehru also wrote a partial autobiography, published in 1936, and a later work that was part historical and part autobiographical, *The Discovery of India,* first published in 1946. He also published a key pamphlet entitled *Whither India?* in 1933. Both men were also inveterate letter writers to friends and colleagues in India and overseas, in an age when our more immediate but ephemeral means of communication were not available. So their communications within their social and professional circles are an important historical source. For both of them the written word was central to working out their perceived predicaments, and their journeys towards identities as modern Indians. Although they were deeply interdependent in personal and professional terms, they also disagreed quite profoundly on some really major issues, and so their friendship, with its discussions, conflicts, and misunderstandings, is particularly illuminating for the historian.

At the outset we must recognise how turbulent and challenging the times were in which Gandhi and Nehru lived. It was hard for thoughtful people to feel at ease with themselves and their environment, and many of them wrestled with deep and urgent problems. The sources of this turbulence were many, but they stemmed in large part from the incorporation of India into the British worldwide empire from the late eighteenth century. The very fact of a colonial government was a challenge to the identity of India and the nature of her polity and society.[1] Moreover, colonial rulers did not hesitate to criticise Indians for their assumed social and political weaknesses, and to argue that colonial rule was both inevitable and providential.[2] British styles of government, at home and in India, as well as their social arrangements, all made Indians think about alternatives that challenged older Indian political and social formations. More particularly the advance of English education was deeply influential. Encouraged by the British for practical and moral purposes, many elite Indians grasped at its availability, just as many had in an earlier age learned Persian, as the language of governance under the Moguls and their successors. But English education provided far more than a common language across the subcontinent. With it came exposure to a whole new spectrum of knowledge and assumptions about society and politics — ranging from Western science, post-Enlightenment understandings of the individual and the state, and the history of Britain's own political and social development, to social sensibilities embedded in English literature. More particularly the British political presence enabled the expansion of Christian missions in India. With the missionaries came fierce critiques of India's religious traditions, and also the social example of humanitarian work for the poor and the underprivileged, especially women.[3] This combination of criticism, pressure, and example in so many areas of public and private life forced sensitive Indians to ask themselves a wide variety of questions. Most obviously they began to interrogate the public and political identity and state of India. Why had the British come to rule India? How could they be removed? What sort of government could replace imperial rule, and what sort of political community might come into being? Indians debated urgently the nature of an Indian nation, past, present, and future, and the suitability of democratic forms of government to forward the life of this nation. In relation to their more private worlds as well as their public identities they questioned their own spiritual and cultural inheritance, wrestling with their religious traditions and the nature of religious authority, and intertwined with this the nature of their social arrangements, particularly the caste hierarchy and established gender norms.[4]

How did Gandhi and Nehru deal with these turbulent times and resolve in their inner worlds some of these issues? Let us look first at their own inner struggles in relation to the nature of the Indian polity, the presence of an imperial ruler, and the extent to which Indian traditions might provide a key to the future. Both men addressed the question whose repercussions confronted them daily: why had India submitted to colonial rule, and how could a handful of foreigners continue to govern India? For both of them British rule was deeply demeaning, whatever the practical benefits it might have brought to some Indians. As Nehru put it, he became obsessed with the thought of India, and driven by "pride, both individual and national, and the desire, common to all men, to resist another's domination and have freedom to live the life of our choice. It seemed to me monstrous that a great country like India, with a rich and immemorial past, should be bound hand and foot to a far-away island which imposed its will upon her. It was more monstrous that this forcible union had resulted in poverty and degradation beyond measure."[5] For Gandhi the problem of colonial rule lay even deeper, in the moral repercussions of British domination. In *Hind Swaraj* he told his reader that the condition of India made him desperately sad—in contrast to the anger of a Nehru. His quarrel with British rule was not so much to do with political justice but with the nature of civilisation the British brought with them. "It is my deliberate opinion that India is being ground down not under the English heel but under that of modern civilisation. It is groaning under the monster's terrible weight."[6] That civilisation, in his understanding, was built on industrialisation, whose techniques were essentially violent, and which in turn assumed that the primary goal of life was material gain. For Gandhi this was a terrible denial of what he assumed to be India's own civilisation built on a more harmonious small-scale way of life rooted in India's villages.

For both Gandhi and Nehru the problem of British imperialism was both inner and outer. It clearly moulded the outer world in which they lived. But it impinged on their inner lives. In part this was because of the destructive and corrosive way it affected their sense of self. It demeaned them, as Nehru had said. But it also challenged their idea of being Indian, as both believed that Indians were responsible for their own degradation and submission to British imperialism. As Gandhi wrote, "The English have not taken India; we have given it up to them. They are not in India because of their strength, but because we keep them."[7] Indian political and religious divisions gave the British leverage in the first place, and subsequently ongoing divisions and the interests of many Westernised Indians, such as lawyers, helped to keep them there. Of lawyers he wrote that "the greatest injury they have done to the country is that they have tightened the English grip. Do you think that it would be possible for the English to carry on their government without law courts?"[8] Although he would never have used the word *collaborator,* as modern imperial historians do, he recognised that the raj depended on those Indians who chose to cooperate with it, by paid employment, by involvement in the Western professions, and of course by paying their taxes. This lay at the heart of the strategy of withdrawal of cooperation from British political and public institutions which he had commended to Congress in 1920. The practice of noncooperation or civil resistance was in part public theatre, as we noted in the previous chapter, to show Indians, their rulers, and the wider world that Indians could peacefully take control of their own public lives, in defiance of the imperial rule. It was the performance of a new national identity. It was designed to inculcate and demonstrate a new moral courage; but it would also demonstrate the reliance of British rule on Indian cooperation in so many political, professional, and financial ways.

For Nehru the Indian weaknesses that had permitted British rule were rather different from the ones that in Gandhi's eyes had produced a moral crisis with political repercussions. Nehru wrote in the 1940s that India "fell behind in the march of technique, and Europe, which had long been backward in many matters, took the lead in technical progress. Behind this technical progress was the spirit of science and a bubbling life and spirit . . ." Given their new military strength, it was not surprising that Western European nations were able to dominate most of Asia.[9] Or again, "A people who are weak and who are left behind in the march of time invite trouble and ultimately have only themselves to blame."[10] Since the root cause of British domination lay in Indians themselves, then Indians would themselves have to change in order to overturn their status as imperial subjects. Both Gandhi and Nehru were convinced that India had the inner resources to do just this. Gandhi believed that Indians had to return to their ancient and simpler civilisation; while Nehru wrote more poetically of his country's "vast stores of suppressed energy and ability" and his wish to "re-charge the battery of India's spirit and waken her from long slumber."[11]

Both men were of course brought up in a world where it was increasingly assumed that the nation was the largest natural political community, and the one that required a political form and structure if it were to flourish and demonstrate its particular nature. Both were confronted by the reality that the idea of an Indian nation was highly contentious. The British, at least in the nineteenth century, claimed that there was no such thing as an Indian nation: internal divisions were so many and so great that only British rule could provide the political framework and order where minorities, particularly religious minorities, would be secure. Among Indians the identity of the nation was also hotly contested from many quarters. Among the most serious grounds of controversy was whether religion alone could be a proper foundation for nationhood. Some Hindus and Muslims alike claimed that this was so. By contrast Gandhi and Nehru vehemently opposed this diminution of the idea of India: they believed the Indian nation included all who had over centuries settled in India and contributed to its diverse and composite culture. For them the foundations of national identity were broadly cultural and geographical rather than religious. Gandhi insisted as early as 1909 that Hindus, Muslims, Parsis, and Christians, indeed all who had made India their country were fellow countrymen. "In no part of the world are one nationality and one religion synonymous terms: nor has it ever been so in India."[12] Nehru spoke passionately of a composite national identity to which all Indians could contribute, and in which all were equal. When confronted with sharpening divisions between Hindus and Muslims in particular, they both believed that it was the British who had divided Indian against Indian to sustain imperial control.[13]

Where Gandhi and Nehru began to diverge radically was on what should come next, what political shape and form the new India should take which would permit the flourishing of the Indian nation and of Indians as individuals. This in turn reflected their different understanding of the fundamental problem of colonial rule. For Gandhi the real issue was a moral one—both the problem and its solution were moral rather than simply political. According to his vision of freedom, or *swaraj*, Indians should turn their backs on most of what the British had brought with them. They would seek to re-establish a simple society founded on the village community, and would be content with a small-scale economy in which every village produced as much as it could to satisfy its own needs, with the goal of adequacy for all rather than a rising standard of living and a consequent likelihood of increasing inequalities of wealth. He was reported to have said, in one of his characteristically brisk and telling aphorisms, that there was enough in the world for every man's need but not for every man's greed. The most moral political formation that would serve the needs of this simpler, nonacquisitive, and noncompetitive society would be an alliance of village communities.[14] By contrast he thought that the modern state, whether in its national or imperial forms, was predicated upon violence, and denied individuals the chance to control their own lives and thus grow to their full moral stature. Given the particular circumstances of India, he was, however, prepared to accept that as an interim measure when British rule ended, India would become some form of modern democratic state. He had never believed in the morality or utility of political power as commonly understood. This was clear in his hostility to Congress contesting elections and taking office before independence. It coloured his resigned acceptance of the sort of nation-state his colleagues desired to achieve at independence. As he had predicted in *Hind Swaraj,* his fellow Indians really wanted English rule without the Englishman. "You want the tiger's nature, but not the tiger; that is to say, you would make India English, and, when it becomes English, it will be called not Hindustan but Englistan. This is not the Swaraj I want."[15]

By contrast, Nehru was, like the vast majority of his compatriots, determined to achieve a modern, democratic nation-state for India. In his view, only this would allow Indians to become free and equal citizens, and give an independent government the authority to use the powers of the state to create a new India. For Nehru personally the new India had to be about transforming India socially and economically, as well as politically. He made this clear in a powerful pamphlet written in 1933, entitled *Whither India?*[16] For him the new India's goal must be the end of exploitation—not just the total end of British dominion, but the end of class privilege and vested interest. "Whither India? surely to the great human goal of social and economic equality, to the ending of all exploitation of nation by nation and class by class, to national freedom within the framework of an international cooperative socialist world federation."[17] The only economic base for such a social transformation would, he believed, be that of a modern style of industrialisation, which could generate the wealth and goods to achieve rising standards of living and greater equality. For Nehru political power was vital as the means to achieve such radical reconstruction of Indian society and renewal of her creative spirit.

Given the difference in their goals, it is not surprising that Nehru and Gandhi differed in the means they advocated. Their personal grappling with the question of right modes of action is another indication of the intertwined search for a new sort of Indian personal and national identity. Gandhi's inner struggle to achieve personal authenticity and autonomy hinged on the search for truth. For him truth was ultimate reality and a far better way of describing it than to use the term *God*. He believed that India's past civilisation had permitted this search, and he struggled to find a lifestyle in the twentieth century that would enable him to pursue this goal. He began to achieve it in South Africa as he progressively simplified his lifestyle and moved from living as a successful Westernised lawyer to sharing a simple communal life akin to that in a Hindu ashram with his colleagues and family. This progression was well described, often with self-deprecating humour, in the autobiography he wrote for Indian consumption in the 1920s. We saw in the previous chapter how, on his final return to India in 1915, his simple, even rustic appearance, and his vegetarian food caused considerable comment among more Westernised Indians. Gandhi also took a vow of celibacy in 1906, which, echoing an established theme in Hindu thought, he believed would enhance his spiritual strength and allow him to serve truth where it was to be found in his fellow men.

On a wider canvas he believed that India's national *swaraj* could be achieved only by similar sorts of personal transformations—as people changed their priorities, simplified their lives, and cared for the humblest and poorest in society. If they did so, British rule would in effect become impossible, though the removal of the British was not Gandhi's fundamental priority. Near the end of his life in 1941 he wrote a pamphlet that summed up all he had been trying to teach his colleagues and countrymen, *Constructive Programme: Its Meaning and Place*.[18] It dealt with a wide range of social issues such as the treatment of women and Untouchables, the benefits of spinning, village industries, education, and communal unity. For him these were the reality of *swaraj*. In the broader project of searching for truth, Gandhi concluded that in any sort of conflict nonviolence was the only moral means, the only way to enable all parties in a conflict to see and achieve Truth. For him ends and means were inextricable; and only by using the right means could individuals and nations achieve moral goals.

He had asserted this as early as 1909 in *Hind Swaraj.* "The means may be likened to a seed, the end to a tree; and there is just the same inviolable connection between the means and the end as there is between the seed and the tree."[19] From this flowed his long-term search for nonviolent means of change, including the practice of *satyagraha* on a national, local, domestic, or personal scale. It was not just a useful strategy but an essential quality of moral action, and at the core of his vision of himself and his life's work.

By contrast Nehru shared neither Gandhi's goal nor his total commitment to nonviolence. We have already seen that he envisaged a socialist India that would put an end to domestic exploitation. Consequently some of his practical priorities echoed Gandhi's. But their ultimate vision of *swaraj* and the new nation's life was quite different. Moreover, Nehru did not view nonviolence in the same way. He believed that it had proved a powerful weapon in their national struggle, but for him it was fundamentally a means of coercion rather than the only way for the individual to pursue truth. He acknowledged that it was probably "the most civilised and moral method [of coercion] and it avoids as far as possible the unpleasant reactions and consequences of violence." He liked the idea of nonviolence and thought it was particularly suited to the particular conditions in which India was placed. However, for him "non-violence is no infallible creed . . . and although I greatly prefer it to violence, I prefer freedom with violence to subjection with non-violence."[20] These large issues to do with the meaning of *swaraj,* the ways to achieve it, and the place of nonviolence were at the heart of many tough debates Gandhi and Nehru had together.[21] Their differences never broke their friendship and their political alliance. Nehru tended to defer to Gandhi at times of crisis in their relationship, but it was his vision and priorities that ultimately dominated the life of the new India rather than the Mahatma's.

As we noted earlier in this chapter, the turmoil in the inner worlds of many thoughtful Indians did not just involve their responses to public and political dilemmas. It also extended to much more personal and intimate areas of life. Again the life histories of Gandhi and

Nehru are a window into many of these issues. (Remember how in our discussion of the Indian family we witnessed Gandhi, the child bridegroom, anxiously reading pamphlets about marriage; and saw how Nehru kicked against the practice of having his marriage arranged to someone he might not even know.) At the heart of much contemporary debate in the nineteenth and twentieth centuries was the nature and role of India's religious traditions. The overt Christian missionary challenge was one reason for this. But the debates occurred also because religious tradition impinged on so many aspects of Indian life, ranging from family relationships and roles, the treatment of women, and the observance of caste, to the public definition of national identity. It was impossible to think about change in society or the creation of a new national identity without also asking questions about religious truth and authority. A huge spectrum of attitudes developed, and Gandhi and Nehru stood in very different places along that spectrum. Consequently their personal struggles and resolution of problems are most instructive for anyone wishing to understand shifts in understandings and sensibilities at this time.

Nehru is perhaps the simpler to understand from a Western perspective. He was brought up in a household where the menfolk at least paid little attention to Hinduism, though concessions were made to the older women's sensibilities, as in the case of having a special kitchen where Indian food could be appropriately cooked, or providing for various Hindu ceremonies. His father did not take their inherited Hindu tradition seriously, and their Kashmiri Brahman community was itself becoming less conservative and more heterodox.[22] In course of time the younger Nehru threw off even the vestiges of Hindu belief and practice, not even wanting to attend family weddings that were performed according to religious rites. Through most of his adult life he believed that rationality should be the criterion for behaviour as a person or as part of a national group. He decried the causes to which religion had been harnessed, whether the subjection of women within the family and their exclusion from public life, or the articulation of a nation in the name of religion, either by Muslims or Hindus. Prioritizing religious identity in public life and belonging was in his view a medieval stance, outmoded by a new rationalism that in turn bred a democratic stance. In particular religion seemed to him a cloak for vested interests or the preserve of the masses whom he saw as uneducated and still in the grip of irrational modes of argument. He wrote in the 1940s, "The outstanding fact seems to me how, on both sides, the communal leaders represent a small upper class reactionary group, and how these people exploit and take advantage of the religious passions of the masses for their own ends. On both sides every effort is made to suppress and avoid the consideration of economic issues."[23] Nehru was perhaps on the further end of the spectrum of contemporary opinion, with those who were self-consciously secular in personal life, and believed that the public life of the new nation should also be secular in the sense of treating all religions equally and giving all equal rights as citizens. Much of his energy as Prime Minister was taken up with combating the persistence of a Hindu interpretation of national identity, and trying to ensure that minorities received equal treatment. As we saw in the previous chapter he was often unsuccessful.

Gandhi by contrast was brought up in a more conservative and pious Vaishnava Hindu household, though his father had numerous friends of other traditions. But as in Nehru's case, for Gandhi Hinduism was a social matter rather than a source of personal inspiration and belief. As he met devout men and women who were Christians, Jews, and Muslims in England and then in South Africa, he was forced to revisit his own tradition and to read for the first time some of the Hindu scriptures. He experienced acute inner turmoil and questioning; as he later wrote, he had gone to South Africa for quite material reasons but found himself "in search of God and striving for self-realization."[24] When he emerged from this time of turmoil after ten years in South Africa it was as a very different kind of man. He continued to call himself a Hindu, and continued to find Hindu tradition and scripture a powerful inspiration, particularly the Bhagavad Gita. But he was no conservative Hindu like some in India, and recognised the inspiration present in other religious traditions. He had come to an understanding of religion beyond and beneath particular traditions—and he would say that there were as many religions as there were individuals. For him true religion was the search for truth, which in turn meant living a life of disciplined simplicity, denial of self, and the service of others, particularly the poor, in whom God was to be found. As he famously wrote in the conclusion to his autobiography, "To see the universal and all-pervading spirit of Truth face to face one must be able to love the meanest of creation as oneself. And a man who aspires after that cannot afford to keep out of any field of life. This is why my devotion to Truth has drawn me into the field of politics; and I can say without the slightest hesitation, and yet in all humility, that those who say that religion has nothing to do with politics do not know what religion means."[25]

Gandhi's understanding of true religion meant that he was free to engage with and challenge many of the contemporary social practices that were justified in the name of religion. He did this in his domestic life as well as in his exhortations on the meaning of real *swaraj*. For example, he criticised many of the practices curtailing the lives of women and treating their lives as less valuable than those of men. He condemned purdah, child marriage, and the restrictions on widow remarriage, particularly as these affected child brides. He urged families to value their daughters as highly as their sons and to educate them. Women were welcomed on equal terms into his own ashram communities, and he encouraged women to participate publicly in the nationalist movement.[26] In the context of political involvement it is significant that he suggested special public roles for women—particularly leading the boycott of foreign cloth and of liquor—thus giving his female colleagues and followers respectable, indeed highly moral, roles. This should warn us against viewing him as some proto-feminist. Although he believed in the equality of men and women as humans and as truth seekers, he still suggested that they had fundamentally different roles in life; but that the two complemented each other.

Similarly Gandhi campaigned against caste as practised in India, and particularly against the practice of untouchability. For him treating people as essentially different, and particularly outcasting and ill-treating Untouchables was a denial of true religion. Moreover, he believed it was not an essential part of Hinduism and was profoundly harmful to that tradition. As he said in 1927, he was deeply hurt by untouchability as he considered himself a Hindu but could find no warrant for untouchability in the Hindu scriptures. Indeed, if he did find such a warrant, "I should have no hesitation in renouncing Hinduism itself. For I hold that religion, to be worthy of the name, must not be inconsistent with the fundamental truths of ethics and morality. But as I believe that untouchability is no part of Hinduism, I cling to Hinduism, but daily become more and more impatient of this hideous wrong."[27] In South Africa he had welcomed people of any religious, ethnic, or caste background into his home communities, nearly causing a rift with his wife in the process. But his campaign on this issue in India itself started in his newly founded ashram in Ahmedabad when he admitted an Untouchable family soon after his return to India. His passionate battle against the practice took him thereafter into several prolonged fasts of protest, and a huge outpouring of writing on the issue, as well as the foundation of a society for Untouchable uplift.[28] The British even offered him facilities to pursue this social campaign while he was in prison in the early 1930s — mainly because they hoped it would deflect him and his followers from the political cause of civil disobedience. Such critiques of social customs claiming religious sanctions brought Gandhi up against the issue of religious authority, which so profoundly troubled many reformers in the India of his day.[29] What was the authority of religious tradition, of scripture, or of religious leaders and functionaries? What could be the basis for arguing for change? Gandhi was clear in his own mind and surprisingly modern. Any practice and any potential change should be judged according to tradition, reason, and conscience, with conscience playing a very significant role. In relation to scripture he was radical — seeing that scripture was in a sense man-made, though no less a source of revelation. Scriptures were a product of their time and place and must be seen as such, and each generation might even produce its own scriptures. It was little wonder that the conservatives saw Gandhi as dangerous and were raucously critical of him.

Nehru, for his part, having rejected Hinduism and indeed any religion as a legitimate source of authority, was also concerned with some of the same problems as Gandhi. But he came from them at a different angle. He was much concerned to transform the lives of Indian women, for example, because he believed—like European radicals and critics of Indian society—that one could judge a society by its treatment of women. The basis for his reformism was rationality, that it was clearly wrong to treat half the national population as inferior, thus depriving human persons of fulfilled lives, and also depriving the nation of their potential contribution to its flourishing. Consequently he argued for the same sort of reforms as Gandhi, and particularly education for girls and young women, so they could take charge of their own lives as autonomous humans. Some of the most significant early reformist legislation of his premiership was to give women a range of civil rights equal to those of men, despite virulent opposition from a range of Hindus.[30] I believe that Nehru's concern for women's rights was also the product of his family experience—taking us back again to the importance of family life histories. While he was in prison during the Second World War his older sister, Vijayalakshmi, was widowed. She only had daughters, and as a result her father-in-law refused to allow her to inherit her husband's personal wealth or his part of the family's wealth. Nehru was scandalised that such a discriminatory custom should rear its head in his own family, but there was little he personally could do about it except assure her that he would look after her. It became a local cause célèbre; and another Kashmiri Brahmin, Sir Tej Bahadur Sapru, friend of their late father's, eminent lawyer, and former Law Member of the Government of India, took up her cause. Although he did not win the case outright he forced the conservative father-in-law to give Vijayalakshmi her husband's personal money. This experience and the profound distress it caused to a sister to whom he was close surely put flesh and blood on this "women's issue" and made compassion join hands with rationality in his subsequent campaign for women's rights. Nehru was less outspoken on matters to do with caste, though his government legislated in 1955 for the abolition of untouchability. For Nehru the theological arguments to do with caste and untouchability were of little interest. Whereas Gandhi took on the conservatives theologically, arguing the case from within Hinduism, Nehru approached the problem as a self-confessed modern man pursuing the goals of equality and socialism. For him the core problem was not religious status but poverty and inequality. The solution rested in the capacity of the new nation-state to relieve poverty by transforming the economy, and to remove inequalities by all means at his disposal. Consequently he was uneasy about Gandhi's campaign against untouchability and the terms in which it was cast; and he deeply disliked Gandhi's apparent glorification of poverty. For Gandhi God was to be found in the poor; for Nehru there should be no poor at all.

This chapter has examined more private and intimate areas of the lives of Gandhi and Nehru, looking not so much at their political work and public roles, but at their inner lives, in particular the way they grappled with some of the most urgent and troubling questions facing Indians of their generations. Of course the inner and the outer were interlinked, and the former provided the spur to much public action. Both men spent their lives on a journey of self-discovery as individuals and as Indians of their time. Both searched for and found very different lode stars, and very different sources of guidance for their lives. Nehru once said that he would always remember Gandhi as a pilgrim figure, staff in hand, striding out to confront wrong and to follow truth. Much the same could have been said about him. He wrote of his own journey of discovering India, geographically and culturally, trying to discover what his country really was, and finding his Indian self through this journey.[31] I find it moving and telling that as Prime Minister he kept on his desk a quotation from Robert Frost which tells of his own sense of journeying as the leader of independent India:

The woods are lovely, dark and deep.
But I have promises to keep,
And miles to go before I sleep.

By attending to the inner lives of two highly significant Indians it has proved possible to have the privilege of hearing these thoughtful and sensitive men discussing their most profound problems and articulating their core ideals. They debated with each other in a relationship of close friendship and political cooperation, but often also when they felt they did not understand each other. Though so very different in background and in the priorities they set themselves, both were fashioning responses to political, ideological, and social issues generated by the presence of the colonial ruler in India and the prospect of freedom and reconstruction. These were serious thinkers as well as activists, not trained philosophers, but men who nonetheless engaged with profound philosophical as well as practical issues. They drew from their knowledge of India and its traditions as well as from the insights of the West and its modes of thought and practice. Ideals and hopes from each entered into dialogue in their minds, enabling them to make new and creative contributions to their country's future. Examining their personal debates, hopes, and fears enriches the historian's understanding of the outer and inner worlds they inhabited, and provides us with evidence about profound issues at stake in India's society and polity in the late nineteenth and early twentieth centuries, many of which continue to confront the peoples of the subcontinent.

Conclusion

The chapters in this volume have explored varieties of "life history" as windows into the past, particularly the recent past of the subcontinent of South Asia and its peoples. To change the metaphor, we have asked whether life history can, at a time of considerable historiographical flux and contestation, be a helpful door or entry point into the historical study of significant themes in the experience of women and men, adding depth and substance to our understanding and arguments, without simplifying the study of the past as older biographies tended to do with their focus on a single life and its influence. We have also considered the possibility that this approach might yield up new historical sources, and offer ways of reading people's experiences beyond the conventional sources of written words.

Chapters 3 and 4 looked at two prominent Indian leaders, Mahatma Gandhi and Jawaharlal Nehru. The approach focused on trying to understand their inner and outer worlds rather than on providing a life narrative. Their experiences in the outer world of public life into which both men entered at a young age yielded up important evidence about the nature of politics on the subcontinent in the late nineteenth and early twentieth centuries. Their recruitment and entry into politics, the diverse roles they played, and the tensions and sometimes heartache they experienced tell the historian much about the political tasks to be done at the level of the aspiring nation and its movement of anticolonial opposition, and then of the newly independent nation-state. They also demonstrate the profound problems facing anyone who trod the road of all-India leadership. Their very different aspirations and political trajectories also shed light on their inner worlds. As historians we have the privilege of overhearing two articulate and thoughtful men grappling individually and together as friends and colleagues with a whole range of intellectual, ideological, religious, and social issues that troubled women and men of their generations as they struggled to understand what it meant to be Indian in the context of colonial rule and Western global domination in the economic and political spheres.

Gandhi and Nehru were of course highly privileged men. They came from families who could afford to send them to England for education and training, and who expected of their male members professional work of one sort or another rather than manual labour. Neither was poor of necessity, and when Gandhi chose a distinctive life of simplicity in his ashram communities it was a life sustained by a serious support organisation and often by the charity of others. Chapter 2 expanded the idea of life history beyond that of the individuals and asked whether examination of individual family histories over time might provide ways of understanding the experience of far less prominent and privileged people, particularly women and those who have migrated from the subcontinent. Focusing on the life history of a family is a possible manoeuvre to gain access to the experiences of people who often did not leave behind more obvious written historical sources, such as letters or autobiographies, and who were, by contrast to some public figures, never conscious of or convinced that they were making history. The patterns of family life over a period of time, including size, gender balance, educational levels, and patterns of physical movement, often enable such people to "speak" to the historian whose ears have been trained to listen. So do photographs, which were increasingly becoming an important mode of family recording and affirmation.

Chapter 1 examined yet another form of life history, pushing and expanding that idea to include the life history of a key educational institution in Britain that came to have a profound influence on relations between Britain and South Asia. We focused on Balliol College, Oxford, notable in the nineteenth and early twentieth centuries for producing generations of British men who went to work in the British Empire, and in India in particular. From the late nineteenth century it also housed and influenced significant numbers of Indian young men who returned to their home country to develop important public roles and careers. This chapter did not provide anything like an institutional history of the college, though it was important to enquire into its ethos and how it came to play this particular public role. The intention was to look at two particular groups of lives spent there and how they subsequently developed. We looked first at the number and sorts of young men who went from Balliol to careers in India, to ask how they were influenced by the relatively short period of time spent there, and to see how that college experience played out in their later careers and complex social relations. In doing so we gained an insight into the working of British imperial rule, and the place of India in the imaginations and interests of the British professional elite. The second group of lives within Balliol were those Indian young men who studied in the college and subsequently returned to India. Through their lives we saw the strong connections between India and some Indians, and part of the British educational system, despite the political opposition within India to British rule, which were to be of considerable and lasting significance for independent India.

These enquiries have suggested the range of sources that historians can use when they focus on life histories of different kinds. They range from more conventional sources such as letters and speeches, diaries and autobiographies, to the potential wealth of information gathered in college registers. They include the evidence of family trees and the changing experience of succeeding generations in such significant areas as the age of marriage, the size of families, and patterns

of education and physical movement, and even the testament of age-
ing family photographs. For the particular history of South Asia, life
histories can provide important insights into many historical themes
and changes: in the fields of imperial and national politics and state-
craft, in the construction and performance of new forms of national
and personal identity, in intellectual and religious contests and transformations, in interpersonal and family relations, and in the emergence of a transnational diaspora of South Asian origin. The evidence
in just this small volume illuminates all these aspects of the experience of the South Asian past. Perhaps one profound insight into that
past has come to dominate our enquiries: recognition of the many
ties that bound India to a far wider world, far earlier than the contemporary experience of globalization. Our diverse lives have shown the
growing importance of foreign travel: of British people to India for
work, of Indians overseas for education, and of Indians who left their
homelands to create new homes overseas, sometimes out of despera-
tion, but often out of a sense of expanding horizons and new opportunities developed as a result of earlier movement within and beyond
India in the context of the British Empire. No one remains unaffected
by foreign travel and by meeting people of different backgrounds and
cultures—as the lives of Gandhi and Nehru both demonstrate. Their
lives were transformed, and so were their understandings of India and
of being Indian. However, even more significant than individual journeys or encounters was the way in which many thousands of Indians
became incorporated into global networks of ideas and ideologies
through education, reading, and sometimes travel and friendship,
as well as by exposure to the British raj and its expatriate personnel.
Nehru and Gandhi were unusual in their levels of contact with people
from other countries and cultures, and also in their voracious reading
habits, as their libraries demonstrate. But many of their compatriots
experienced the novel and the challenging in the nineteenth and twentieth centuries, whether they remained at home or traveled overseas.
In responding to such influences in their private and public lives they
demonstrated the complex and important ways in which the sub-

continent was tied to a far wider world. South Asia's own history cannot be understood without recognition of its long-standing incorporation into global networks of contact and influence. Life histories of different kinds provide evidence of this incorporation and its lasting significance.

Notes

Introduction

1. For a magisterial survey of some of these issues see John Burrow, *A History of Histories: Epics, Chronicles, Romances and Inquiries from Herodotus and Thucydides to the Twentieth Century* (London: Allen Lane, Penguin Books, 2007).

2. The first of this series was published in 1982: R. Guha, ed., *Subaltern Studies I: Writings on South Asian History and Society* (Delhi: Oxford University Press, 1982).

3. E. Said, *Orientalism* (New York: Pantheon Books, 1978).

4. See the essays in the forum on biography, "AHR Roundtable: Historians and Biography," *American Historical Review* 114:3 (2009): 573–661.

5. Judith M. Brown, *Gandhi: Prisoner of Hope* (New Haven: Yale University Press, 1989), and *Nehru: A Political Life* (New Haven: Yale University Press, 2003).

1.   Colleges, Cohorts, and Dynasties

1. Directly relevant to this chapter is a groundbreaking book on the Indian Civil Service. It is a study of several generations of a particular professional group, and the profound continuities between the pre- and post-independence service, which stemmed from the processes of recruitment, training, and broad socialisation of new recruits: D. Potter, *India's Political Administrators, 1919–1983* (Oxford: Clarendon Press, 1986).

A more popular work that examines the generation of British women who never married because of the slaughter of British men during the First World War is V. Nicholson, *Singled Out: How Two Million Women Survived Without Men After the First World War* (London: Penguin Books, 2007). One reviewer described it as a "vivid and moving portrait of a unique generation of women."

2. On this calculation and the social realities flowing from it see E. Buettner, *Empire Families: Britons and Late Imperial India* (Oxford: Oxford University Press, 2004). A poignant memoir of a family separated by this perceived social need over the generations they spent in India is I. Macfarlane, *Daughters of the Empire: A Memoir of Life and Times in the British Raj* (New Delhi: Oxford University Press, 2006). On the public schools see D. Newsome, *Godliness and Good Learning: Four Studies on a Victorian Ideal* (London: John Murray, 1961).

3. See, for example, two volumes edited by J. A. Mangan in the Manchester Studies in Imperialism series: *"Benefits Bestowed"? Education and British Imperialism* (Manchester: Manchester University Press, 1988); *Making Imperial Mentalities: Socialisation and British Imperialism* (Manchester: Manchester University Press, 1990).

4. See B. N. Ramusack, *The Indian Princes and Their States* (Cambridge: Cambridge University Press, 2004), 111.

5. I am indebted for discussion of this school to a research seminar in Oxford on 27 October 2006 by Professor T. Chafer of Southampton University.

6. Minute by Lord Canning, 29 October 1860, cited in Buettner, *Empire Families,* 77. People of mixed descent proved exceptionally useful to the British in areas such as the railways and the postal and telegraph services, where their fluency in English and technical skills, and their loyalty and aspirations for acceptance as European were of particular importance.

7. See the work on the Doon School by the anthropologist Sanjay Srivastava, *Constructing Post-Colonial India: National Character and the Doon School* (London: Routledge, 1998).

8. For a good introduction to the old networks of patronage and the emergence of families with connections with India generation by generation ("dolphin families," echoing Rudyard Kipling), see chap. 1 of D. Gilmour, *The Ruling Caste: Imperial Lives in the Victorian Raj* (London: John Murray, 2005).

9. See tables in the appendix of R. Symonds, *Oxford and Empire: The Last Lost Cause?* (Oxford: Clarendon Press, 1991).

10. See J. Jones, *Balliol College: A History*, 2nd ed., rev. (Oxford: Oxford University Press, 2005), particularly 174 ff.

11. Ibid., 226.

12. Gilmour, *The Ruling Caste*, 62.

13. See app. E in Jones, *Balliol College*, 331.

14. There has been considerably scholarly attention to the nature of the ICS examination and the systems of recruitment. For an overview see Gilmour, *The Ruling Caste*, chap. 2, "Competition Wallahs"—this being the somewhat pejorative term given by old India hands to the new generation who entered service via the competition. One of the new generation himself wrote of the products of the crammers, "They neither ride, nor shoot, nor dance, nor play cricket, and prefer the companionship of their books to the attraction of Indian society." Cited in Gilmour, *The Ruling Caste*, 63. Other significant works are J. M. Compton, "Open Competition and the Indian Civil Service, 1854–1876," *English Historical Review* 83 (April 1968): 265–84; B. Spangenburg, "The Problem of Recruitment for the Indian Civil Service in the Later Nineteenth Century," *Journal of Asian Studies* 30 (1971): 341–60; C. Dewey, "The Education of a Ruling Caste: The Indian Civil Service in the Era of the Competitive Examination," *English Historical Review* 88 (April 1973): 262–85.

15. Jones, *Balliol College*, 218. The probationers were given their own tutor, initially Arnold Toynbee. Later they were cared for in Balliol by Sir William Markby, a Fellow and Reader in Indian law in the university: he had had a distinguished career in India as a judge in the Calcutta High Court and as Vice Chancellor of Calcutta University. He was a Fellow of Balliol from 1883 to 1914.

16. See part 5 of H. Ellis, "Proconsuls, Guardians and Greats Men: The Rulers of British India and an Education in Empire: 1880–1914" (B.A. thesis in Ancient and Modern History, Oxford University, 2002).

17. On the very significant problems in recruiting Europeans to the ICS after 1919 see Potter, *India's Political Administrators, 1919–1983*, particularly 83 ff.

18. The role of the European ICS man was under various pressures after the 1914–18 war, particularly growing Indianization of the service, the devolution of political power to Indians through successive constitutional reforms, and nationalist hostility to the front line of imperial rule. Although a significant number of older ICS men took early retirement after the 1919 constitutional reforms, many continued to find it an interesting and desirable career. See for example the letters home of a young man from Trinity College,

Cambridge: W. H. Saumarez Smith, *A Young Man's Country: Letters of a Subdivisional Officer of the Indian Civil Service, 1936–1937* (Salisbury: Michael Russell, 1977). His final letter home reflecting on his sixteen months in Madaripur, Bengal, his first charge, concluded, "I left Madaripur with mixed feelings. I can't say my sixteen months there have been exactly happy, but they have been intensely interesting" (99).

19. Gilmour, *The Ruling Caste,* 29–32.

20. His descendents deposited his photo albums in the college library where they are a wonderful record of the social and working life of an ICS man. He was interestingly one of those who passed the entrance examination to the ICS despite a less than distinguished academic record: he gained a second class in his part 1 and a third in part 2 (classics).

21. There is a well-developed literature on gender and empire. See P. Levine, ed., *Gender and Empire* (Oxford: Oxford University Press, 2004).

22. A vivid account of his student experience in London can be found in M. K. Gandhi, *An Autobiography: The Story of My Experiments with Truth* (1927; London: Jonathan Cape, 1966). Jawaharlal Nehru had an easier passage to Cambridge as he had already been at boarding school in England, at Harrow. See his *An Autobiography* (London: John Lane, The Bodley Head, 1936). An important analysis of Indian student life in England in the early twentieth century is S. Mukherjee, "The Experience of the 'England-Returned': The Education of Indians in Britain in the Early Twentieth Century and Its Long-Term Impact" (D. Phil. thesis, Oxford University, 2007).

23. Jones, *Balliol College,* 219.

24. See the memoirs of Cornelia Sorabji, *India Calling: The Memories of Cornelia Sorabji, India's First Woman Barrister,* ed. C. Lokuge (1934; New Delhi: Oxford University Press, 2001).

25. I owe this communal college memory to Dr. John Jones. He also told me that when *Sanders of the River* (1935) was showing in the cinema a Trinity man greeted a scene of Africans rowing with the cry "Well rowed, Balliol." This would tie in with the greater flow of Indians into Balliol in the 1930s mentioned below.

26. This point was made in relation to the ICS by Potter in his *India's Political Administrators,* 144–45, and he notes the critical reaction by some Indians to these fast promotions. Potter does not mention those who prospered by transferring to the Foreign Service. It would be interesting to know if this was a peculiarly Balliol phenomenon!

2.   *Family Histories*

1.   Buettner, *Empire Families*.

2.   In 2007, for example, the BBC series *Who Do You Think You Are?* featured the actor Alistair McGowan. He thought he was of Scottish descent, but when his father died he noted that on his birth certificate his father was recorded as "Anglo-Indian." Following this clue, the programme traced direct McGowan ancestors and kin who were in fact Eurasian, living in India. They were descended from an Irish soldier who had joined the army of the East India Company in the 1780s; he had married a local woman with a Portuguese name who may have been of mixed descent herself, and their grandson married a Muslim woman of standing in northern India. See www.bbcwhodoyouthinkyouare.com/stories.

3.   See, for example, B. Caine, *Bombay to Bloomsbury: A Biography of the Strachey Family* (Oxford: Oxford University Press, 2005).

4.   This was a family of Khatris from the western Punjab of united India, and a family member who later became a senior manager in an Indian company wrote an entrancing memoir of three generations of his family: P. Tandon, *Punjabi Century, 1857–1947* (London: Chatto & Windus, 1963). He wrote subsequent volumes that took his story beyond 1947.

5.   J. A. P. Majumdar, *Family History,* ed. A. Burton (New Delhi: Oxford University Press, 2003). A retired colleague of my own at Oxford, Professor Tapan Raychaudhuri, has written his memoirs in Bengali. They contain a considerable amount on his family and its Bengali background, and some valuable family photographs. Professor Bharati Ray of the University of Calcutta has studied the women of her grandmother's generation.

6.   Buettner, *Empire Families*. For a memoir of one such family see I. Macfarlane, *Daughters of the Empire*.

7.   Brij V. Lal, *On the Other Side of Midnight: A Fijian Journey* (New Delhi: National Book Trust, India, 2005). On his grandfather's own experience of indenture, and his personal return to his grandfather's village in northern India, see chap. 2, "Return to Bahraich," in Brij V. Lal, *Chalo Jahaji on a Journey Through Indenture in Fiji* (Suva: Australian National University, Canberra & Fiji Museum, 2000).

8.   A convenient introduction to some of this literature is in Burton's introduction to Majumdar, *Family History*. See also the groundbreaking essay by T. Raychaudhuri, "Love in a Colonial Climate: Marriage, Sex and Romance in Nineteenth-century Bengal," in his *Perceptions, Emotions, Sensibilities:*

Essays on India's Colonial and Post-colonial Experiences (New Delhi: Oxford University Press, 1999), chap. 4.

9. J. Majeed, *Autobiography, Travel and Postnational Identity: Gandhi, Nehru and Iqbal* (Houndmills, Basingstoke: Palgrave Macmillan, 2007).

10. M. K. Gandhi, *An Autobiography: The Story of My Experiments with Truth*.

11. J. Nehru, *An Autobiography*, 7. See also V. L. Pandit, *The Scope of Happiness: A Personal Memoir* (London: Weidenfeld & Nicolson, 1979).

12. See chap 1 of C. Sorabji, *India Calling*.

13. These new literary forms are discussed as emerging in different social and religious contexts in India by M. Borthwick, *The Changing Role of Women in Bengal, 1849–1905* (Princeton: Princeton University Press, 1985), and G. Minault, *Secluded Scholars: Women's Education and Muslim Social Reform in Colonial India* (New Delhi: Oxford University Press, 1998).

14. A pioneering collection of translations of female writings is S. Tharu and K. Lalita, eds., *Women Writing in India*, 2 vols. (London: Pandora Press, 1991, 1993).

15. See review article by Sophie Gordon, "Photography in India," *IIAS Newletter* (Summer 2007): 10–11, with suggestions for further reading. A groundbreaking work was C. Pinney, *Camera Indica: The Social Life of Indian Photographs* (London: Reaktion Press, 1997). See M. Karlekar, ed., *Visualizing Indian Women, 1875–1947* (New Delhi: Oxford University Press, 2006), dealing specifically with the way the new photographic techniques came to depict women.

16. In addition to the two discussed in detail, many are beautifully reproduced in Karlekar, *Visualizing Indian Women*. See particularly those in the chapter "Showcasing the Family" and the accompanying text.

17. See the selection of photographs of married couples in Karlekar, *Visualizing Indian Women*, 4–11.

18. See, for example, P. Thompson, *The Voice of the Past: Oral History*, 3rd ed. (1978; Oxford: Oxford University Press, 2000).

19. A major milestone in this development was the publication in the series the New Cambridge History of India of G. Forbes, *Women in Modern India* (Cambridge: Cambridge University Press, 1996). This has an important bibliography.

20. See n. 6, above. More broadly on gender and imperial history see R. O'Hanlon, "Gender in the British Empire," chap. 16 of Judith M. Brown and William Roger Louis, eds., *The Oxford History of the British Empire*, vol. 4,

The Twentieth Century (Oxford: Oxford University Press, 1999); P. Levine, *Gender and Empire.*

21. The evidence of the "missing millions" of Indian women is clear from the decennial census in India. Many baby girls and female foetuses are deliberately destroyed for cultural reasons to do with the greater worth accorded to boys as well as the financial burden of girls. This phenomenon is not confined to the poorest states but is clearly visible in ones that have done well out of modern economic advance, such as the Punjab. According to the 2001 Census of India, for every 1000 men there were 933 women in India as a whole. However, in Punjab and Haryana respectively the figure for women was 874 and 861; neither can be called a poor state. By contrast, in Kerala, with its large Christian population and virtually total literacy for men and women, there were 1,058 women for every 1000 men. The profound problem of the "missing millions" was highlighted in B. D. Miller, *The Endangered Sex* (Ithaca: Cornell University Press, 1981); and in an article by Amartya Sen, "More Than 100 Million Women Are Missing," *The New York Review,* 10 December 1990, which discussed India and China.

22. See Judith M. Brown, *Nehru: A Political Life,* 42–43.

23. J. Nehru to Indira Nehru, 9 July 1941, *Selected Works of Jawaharlal Nehru,* series 1, ed. S. Gopal (New Delhi: Orient Longman, 1972–82), 11:643–48.

24. Brown, *Nehru: A Political Life,* 100.

25. There is no satisfactory biography of Indira Gandhi (née Nehru), partly because access to her personal papers is not permitted. The most serious attempt is M. Frank, *Indira: The Life of Indira Nehru Gandhi* (London: HarperCollins, 2001).

26. It would be instructive to see if this strategy of constructing longitudinal life histories of families could be used for other "subaltern" groups, such as Untouchables or converts to Christianity in India, who often came from such lowly groups in society.

27. There is a rich literature on indentured labour, both the system and the experiences of those caught up in this type of labour relationship. For an introduction see D. Northrup, *Indentured Labor in the Age of Imperialism, 1834–1922* (Cambridge: Cambridge University Press, 1995). See also the works of B. V. Lal, who is referred to above, n. 7.

28. For an introduction see my *Global South Asians: Introducing the Modern Diaspora* (Cambridge: Cambridge University Press, 2006).

29. See http://www.movinghere.org.uk/. Another interesting Internet source is the account of a Sikh family's diaspora movements and connections

written by an amateur historian of his own community: www.sikhglobalvillage
.com. Unfortunately even where research over several generations has been
conducted it has not been of experiences within the same family. See J. Eade
et al., *Tales of Three Generations of Bengalis in Britain* (London: Nirmul Committee, 2006).

30. See, for example, M. H. Fisher, *Counterflows to Colonialism: Indian Travellers and Settlers in Britain, 1600–1857* (Delhi: Permanent Black, 2004).

31. A. N. Halsey and J. Webb, eds., *Twentieth-Century British Social Trends*
(Houndmills, Basingstoke: Macmillan, 2000), 154.

32. In Britain in 1991 the average household size was 2.4 people. For Indians the average was 3.8, for Pakistanis 4.8, and for Bangladeshis 5.3. Ibid., 154.

3.   Individual Lives and Their Public World

1. Brown, *Gandhi: Prisoner of Hope,* and *Nehru: A Political Life.*

2. J. Nehru, *An Autobiography,* 596.

3. See J. Majeed, *Autobiography, Travel and Postnational Identity: Gandhi,
Nehru and Iqbal.* References to the autobiographical works of several Indians,
including those of Gandhi and Nehru, can be found in the notes to chap. 2.

4. See S. Beth, "Hindi Dalit Autobiography: An Exploration of Identity," *Modern Asian Studies* 41:3 (2007): 545–74. Professor Brij Lal's autobiographical work, also referred to in chap. 2, is in some ways similar, as an attempt to understand and refashion a once degraded identity, the indentured
labourer as victim.

5. The Gujarati text of 1909 translated in English is to be found in the
relevant chronological volume of *The Collected Works of Mahatma Gandhi.* An
excellent modern translation with scholarly introduction is by A. J. Parel,
published by Cambridge University Press, Cambridge, 1997.

6. Gandhi's increasing simplification of his personal lifestyle, his vow
of celibacy, and his transformation of his home into a series of ashrams
(Hindu religious communities) are described in detail in his *Autobiography.* A
fairly characteristic response to him by someone who was sympathetic was the
comment by V. S. S. Sastri in a letter to his brother, V. S. R. Sastri, 10 January
1915, in which he expressed surprise at Gandhi's simple traditional clothes,
rather than more formal or Westernised dress, his "queer food" (fruit, nuts,
and no animal products), and the fact that Mrs. Gandhi did not speak English.
See T. N. Jagadisan, ed., *Letters of the Right Honourable V. S. Srinivasa Sastri,* 2nd
ed. (Bombay: Asia Publishing House, 1963), 40.

7. See Nehru's account of this phase of growing dissatisfaction with his life in his *Autobiography,* chap. 5.

8. On the British political strategy of reform see Judith M. Brown, *Modern India: The Origins of an Asian Democracy,* 2nd ed. (Oxford: Oxford University Press, 1994), 195–209.

9. For a detailed analysis of this crucial period in Indian politics, see Judith M. Brown, *Gandhi's Rise to Power: Indian Politics, 1915–1922* (Cambridge: Cambridge University Press, 1972).

10. Nehru, *An Autobiography,* 69.

11. Baring to Mallet, 25 September 1882, cited in A. Seal, *The Emergence of Indian Nationalism: Competition and Collaboration in the Later Nineteenth Century* (Cambridge: Cambridge University Press, 1968), 156.

12. Pant eventually left the state in 1954 at Nehru's request to become Home Minister in the all-India government in Delhi. His career and concerns are well documented in his *Selected Works,* currently being edited by B. R. Nanda and published by Oxford University Press, Delhi. His life awaits serious analysis. The ambiguity of the Congress as both a local and a national organisation and the tensions between the two levels of political activity is well shown in B. R. Tomlinson, *The Indian National Congress and the Raj, 1929–1942: The Penultimate Phase* (London: Macmillan, 1976).

13. On the chaotic or often nonexistent nature of the local Congress organisation in 1929, see Judith M. Brown, *Gandhi and Civil Disobedience: The Mahatma in Indian Politics, 1928–34* (Cambridge: Cambridge University Press, 1977), 48–53.

14. Here the career of Motilal Nehru in the 1920s, and his unsuccessful attempt to run an all-India Swaraj party in the legislatures, is most instructive about the political system at the time. His failures can be contrasted with the phenomenon of the rise of the MLA, the provincial member of the legislative assembly, who increasingly became the fixer in local politics, and the man who could deploy the very real resources available through work in the provincial legislature. The rise of the MLA at the expense of some of the local influence of the local ICS man helped to make an ICS career less attractive to British men after the constitutional reforms of 1919. We saw the clear decline in British recruits in my discussion of Balliol's links with India in chap. 1. See S. Epstein, "District Officers in Decline: The Erosion of British Authority in the Bombay Countryside, 1919 to 1947," *Modern Asian Studies* 16:3 (1982): 493–518.

15. For the details of Gandhi's Indian career see my *Gandhi: Prisoner of Hope,* and the monographs referred to in notes 9 and 13.

16. A study of one particular local *satyagraha* is "Holds Barred: Anatomy of a Satyagraha, Lucknow, May 1930," chap. 3 of D. A. Low, *Britain and Indian Nationalism: The Imprint of Ambiguity, 1929–1942* (Cambridge: Cambridge University Press, 1997).

17. For a detailed study of the Government of India's dilemmas see D. A. Low, "'Civil Martial Law': The Government of India and the Civil Disobedience Movements, 1930–34," chap. 5 of D. A. Low, ed., *Congress and the Raj: Facets of the Indian Struggle, 1917–47,* 2nd ed. (New Delhi: Oxford University Press, 2004).

18. Good examples of this work were when Gandhi in the mid-1930s managed to keep his more conservative colleagues working with Nehru. One of the only examples of Gandhi working to remove a disruptive element from Congress was his response to S. C. Bose in 1938–39.

19. Gandhi's signature can be found in the Master's guestbook, which is still in use today, over seventy years later.

20. The context for this was the alignment of the all-India movement with a particular local movement of peasant protest.

21. Gandhi to Vallabhbhai Patel, 18 April 1934, *The Collected Works of Mahatma Gandhi* (Delhi: Government of India, 1958–84), 57:403–5.

22. Brown, *Nehru: A Political Life,* 78–79.

23. The start of the process is well documented in Tomlinson, *The Indian National Congress and the Raj,* chap. 3. See also the local case studies in M. Weiner, *Party Building in a New Nation: The Indian National Congress* (Chicago: University of Chicago Press, 1967).

24. Nehru's didactic role can be well seen in his public speeches but also in the fascinating run of regular letters to his Chief Ministers. These are included in their chronological place in the *Selected Works of Jawaharlal Nehru,* series 2 (New Delhi: J. Nehru Memorial Fund, 1984–); they are also available separately in five volumes edited by G. Parthasarathi, *Letters to Chief Ministers, 1947–1964* (New Delhi: J. Nehru Memorial Fund, 1985–89).

4. Individual Lives and Their Inner World

1. See chapter 2, "Hindu Responses to British Rule," in B. Parekh, *Colonialism, Tradition and Reform: An Analysis of Gandhi's Political Discourse,* rev. ed. (New Delhi: Sage Publications, 1999). Here Parekh not only examines the tradition of discourse in which Gandhi took his place, but underlines that

many Hindus discussed the "problem" of imperial rule in terms of the nature of their own society and its evident need for regeneration.

2. The British did not elaborate a clear ideology of empire, but a good introduction to some of their attitudes and assumptions about Indians and their own imperial rule is to be found in T. R. Metcalf, *Ideologies of the Raj* (Cambridge: Cambridge University Press, 1994). From a rather different perspective see also C. Dewey, *Anglo-Indian Attitudes: The Mind of the Indian Civil Service* (London: Hambledon Press, 1993).

3. For an overview of the history of Christianity in India see R. E. Frykenberg, *Christianity in India: From Beginnings to the Present* (Oxford: Oxford University Press, 2008). Gandhi was eventually influenced powerfully by Christian teaching, but his first exposure to missionary preaching and their criticism of Hindus and Hinduism offended him deeply. See Gandhi, *An Autobiography,* part 1, chap. 10.

4. See K. W. Jones, *Socio-religious Reform Movements in British India* (Cambridge: Cambridge University Press, 1989); and the essays in part 1 of T. Raychaudhuri, *Perceptions, Emotions, Sensibilities.*

5. J. Nehru, *The Discovery of India* (1946; Bombay: Asia Publishing House, 1960), 36.

6. M. K. Gandhi, *Hind Swaraj,* ed. A. Parel (1909; Cambridge: Cambridge University Press, 1997), 42.

7. Ibid., 39.

8. Ibid., 61.

9. Nehru, *The Discovery of India,* 41.

10. Ibid., 306.

11. Ibid., 43–44. By contrast Gandhi's *Hind Swaraj* had practical prescriptions for the achievement of *swaraj.*

12. Gandhi, *Hind Swaraj,* 52–53.

13. Ibid., p. 48; Nehru, *The Discovery of India,* 305.

14. See Gandhi's explication of this vision in 1942 and 1946, quoted in Judith M. Brown, ed., *Mahatma Gandhi: The Essential Writings,* new ed. (Oxford: Oxford University Press, 2008), 102–4.

15. Gandhi, *Hind Swaraj,* 28. A convenient collection of Gandhi's writings on many of these interlocking issues is Judith M. Brown, ed., *Mahatma Gandhi: The Essential Writings.*

16. *Whither India?* in *Selected Works of Jawaharlal Nehru,* series 1, 6:1–16.

17. Ibid., 16.

18. *The Collected Works of Mahatma Gandhi,* 75:146–66.

19. *Hind Swaraj,* 81.

20. *Whither India?* in *Selected Works of Jawaharlal Nehru,* series 1, 6:25.

21. For example in 1933, when Nehru was released from prison and found civil disobedience in disarray and Gandhi recovering from a fast over work for abolishing untouchability. See Brown, *Nehru: A Political Life,* 111−14.

22. Nehru, *An Autobiography,* chaps. 2 and 3.

23. Ibid., 467−68.

24. Gandhi, *An Autobiography,* 132.

25. Ibid., 420.

26. For a selection of Gandhi's writings on issues to do with women see Brown, ed., *Mahatma Gandhi: The Essential Writings,* 228−58.

27. Speech in Trivandrum, reported in his paper, *Young India,* 20 October 1927, ibid., 214.

28. A selection of Gandhi's pronouncements on untouchability are to be found in ibid., 210−28.

29. See K. W. Jones, *Socio-religious Reform Movements in British India.*

30. See R. Som, "Jawaharlal Nehru and the Hindu Code: A Victory of Symbol over Substance?" *Modern Asian Studies* 28:1 (1994): 165−94.

31. Nehru, *The Discovery of India,* e.g., 36−39.

Sources

Primary Sources

The Balliol College Registers. Several editions of these have been published in the course of the twentieth and twenty-first centuries, mainly for private circulation, and it is necessary to use successive ones to track individual lives. A complete set is available in the college library in Oxford.

Gandhi, M. K. *Hind Swaraj.* In *Gandhi: Hind Swaraj and Other Writings,* edited by A. Parel. 1909. Cambridge: Cambridge University Press, 1997.

———. *An Autobiography: The Story of My Experiments with Truth.* 1927. London: Jonathan Cape, 1966.

———. *The Collected Works of Mahatma Gandhi.* Delhi: Government of India, 1958–84.

———. *Mahatma Gandhi: The Essential Writings.* New ed. Edited by Judith M. Brown. Oxford: Oxford University Press, 2008.

Jagadisan, T. N., ed. *Letters of the Right Honourable V. S. Srinivasa Sastri.* 2nd ed. Bombay: Asia Publishing House, 1963.

Macfarlane, I. *Daughters of the Empire: A Memoir of Life and Times in the British Raj.* New Delhi: Oxford University Press, 2006.

Majumdar, J. A. P. *Family History.* Edited by A. Burton. New Delhi: Oxford University Press, 2003.

Nehru, J. *An Autobiography.* London: John Lane, The Bodley Head, 1936.

———. *The Discovery of India.* 1946. Bombay: Asia Publishing House, 1960.

———. *Selected Works of Jawaharlal Nehru.* Series 1. Edited by S. Gopal. New Delhi: Orient Longman, 1972–82.

———. *Selected Works of Jawaharlal Nehru.* Series 2. Edited by S. Gopal, R. Kumar, and H. Prasad. New Delhi: J. Nehru Memorial Fund, 1984–.

———. *Letters to Chief Ministers, 1947–1964.* 5 vols. Edited by G. Parthasarathi. New Delhi: J. Nehru Memorial Fund, 1985–89.

Pandit, V. *The Scope of Happiness: A Personal Memoir.* London: Weidenfeld & Nicolson, 1979.

Pant, G. B. *Selected Works of Govind Ballabh Pant.* Edited by B. R. Nanda. Delhi: Oxford University Press, 1993–.

Saumarez Smith, W. H. *A Young Man's Country: Letters of a Subdivisional Officer of the Indian Civil Service, 1936–1937.* Salisbury: Michael Russell, 1977.

Sorabji, C. *India Calling: The Memories of Cornelia Sorabji, India's First Woman Barrister.* Edited by C. Lokuge. 1934. New Delhi: Oxford University Press, 2001.

Tandon, P. *Punjabi Century, 1857–1947.* London: Chatto & Windus, 1963.

Tharu, S., and K. Lalita, eds. *Women Writing in India.* 2 vols. London: Pandora Press, 1991, 1993.

Websites: www.movinghere.org.uk, www.sikhglobalvillage.com, www.bbc whodoyouthinkyouare.com/stories.

Secondary Sources

"AHR Roundtable: Historians and Biography." *American Historical Review* 114:3 (2009): 573–661.

Beth, S. "Hindi Dalit Autobiography: An Exploration of Identity." *Modern Asian Studies* 41:3 (2007): 545–74.

Borthwick, M. *The Changing Role of Women in Bengal, 1849–1905.* Princeton: Princeton University Press, 1985.

Brown, Judith M. *Gandhi's Rise to Power: Indian Politics, 1915–1922.* Cambridge: Cambridge University Press, 1972.

———. *Gandhi and Civil Disobedience: The Mahatma in Indian Politics, 1928–34.* Cambridge: Cambridge University Press, 1977.

———. *Gandhi: Prisoner of Hope.* New Haven: Yale University Press, 1989.

———. *Modern India: The Origins of an Asian Democracy.* 2nd ed. Oxford: Oxford University Press, 1994.

———. *Nehru: A Political Life.* New Haven: Yale University Press, 2003.

————. *Global South Asians: Introducing the Modern Diaspora*. Cambridge: Cambridge University Press, 2006.

————. "'Life Histories' and the History of Modern South Asia." AHR Roundtable: Historians and Biography. *American Historical Review* 114 (2009): 587–95.

Brown, Judith M., and William Roger Louis, eds. *The Oxford History of the British Empire*. Vol. 4, *The Twentieth Century*. Oxford: Oxford University Press, 1999.

Buettner, E. *Empire Families: Britons and Late Imperial India*. Oxford: Oxford University Press, 2004.

Burrow, J. *A History of Histories: Epics, Chronicles, Romances and Inquiries from Herodotus and Thucydides to the Twentieth Century*. London: Allen Lane, Penguin Books, 2007.

Caine, B. *Bombay to Bloomsbury: A Biography of the Strachey Family*. Oxford: Oxford University Press, 2005.

Compton, J. M. "Open Competition and the Indian Civil Service, 1854–1876." *English Historical Review* 83 (April 1968): 265–84.

Dewey, C. "The Education of a Ruling Caste: The Indian Civil Service in the Era of the Competitive Examination." *English Historical Review* 88 (April 1973): 262–85.

————. *Anglo-Indian Attitudes: The Mind of the Indian Civil Service*. London: Hambledon Press, 1993.

Eade, J., with A. A. Ullah, J. Iqbal, and M. Hey. *Tales of Three Generations of Bengalis in Britain*. London: Nirmul Committee, 2006.

Ellis, H. "Proconsuls, Guardians and Greats Men: The Rulers of British India and an Education in Empire, 1880–1914." B.A. thesis in Ancient and Modern History, Oxford University, 2002.

Epstein, S. "District Officers in Decline: The Erosion of British Authority in the Bombay Countryside, 1919 to 1947." *Modern Asian Studies* 16:3 (1982): 493–518.

Fisher, M. H. *Counterflows to Colonialism: Indian Travellers and Settlers in Britain, 1600–1857*. Delhi: Permanent Black, 2004.

Forbes, G. *Women in Modern India*. Cambridge: Cambridge University Press, 1996.

Frank, M. *Indira: The Life of Indira Nehru Gandhi*. London: HarperCollins, 2001.

Frykenberg, R. E. *Christianity in India: From Beginnings to the Present*. Oxford: Oxford University Press, 2008.

Gilmour, D. *The Ruling Caste: Imperial Lives in the Victorian Raj.* London: John Murray, 2005.

Gordon, S. "Photography in India." *IIAS Newsletter* (Summer 2007): 10–11.

Guha, R., ed. *Subaltern Studies I: Writings on South Asian History and Society.* Delhi: Oxford University Press, 1982.

Halsey. A. N., and J. Webb, eds. *Twentieth-Century British Social Trends.* Houndmills, Basingstoke: Macmillan, 2000.

Jones, J. *Balliol College: A History.* 2nd ed., rev. Oxford: Oxford University Press, 2005.

Jones, K. W. *Socio-religious Reform Movements in British India.* Cambridge: Cambridge University Press, 1989.

Karlekar, M., ed. *Visualizing Indian Women, 1875–1947.* New Delhi: Oxford University Press, 2006.

Lal, B. V. *Chalo Jahaji on a Journey Through Indenture in Fiji.* Suva: Australian National University, Canberra & Fiji Museum, 2000.

———. *On the Other Side of Midnight: A Fijian Journey.* New Delhi: National Book Trust, India, 2005.

Levine, P., ed. *Gender and Empire.* Oxford: Oxford University Press, 2004.

Low, D. A. *Britain and Indian Nationalism: The Imprint of Ambiguity, 1929–1942.* Cambridge: Cambridge University Press, 1997.

———, ed. *Congress and the Raj: Facets of the Indian Struggle, 1917–47.* 2nd ed. New Delhi: Oxford University Press, 2004.

Majeed, J. *Autobiography, Travel and Postnational Identity: Gandhi, Nehru and Iqbal.* Houndmills, Basingstoke: Palgrave Macmillan, 2007.

Mangan, J. A., ed. *"Benefits Bestowed"? Education and British Imperialism.* Manchester: Manchester University Press, 1988.

———. *Making Imperial Mentalities: Socialisation and British Imperialism.* Manchester: Manchester University Press, 1990.

Metcalf, T. R. *Ideologies of the Raj.* Cambridge: Cambridge University Press, 1994.

Miller, B. D. *The Endangered Sex.* Ithaca: Cornell University Press, 1981.

Minault, G. *Secluded Scholars: Women's Education and Muslim Social Reform in Colonial India.* New Delhi: Oxford University Press, 1998.

Mukherjee, S. "The Experience of the 'England-Returned': The Education of Indians in Britain in the Early Twentieth Century and Its Long-Term Impact." D. Phil. thesis, Oxford University, 2007.

Newsome, D. *Godliness and Good Learning: Four Studies on a Victorian Ideal.* London: John Murray, 1961.

Nicholson, V. *Singled Out: How Two Million Women Survived Without Men After the First World War.* London: Penguin Books, 2007.

Northrup, D. *Indentured Labour in the Age of Imperialism, 1834–1922.* Cambridge: Cambridge University Press, 1995.

Parekh, B. *Colonialism, Tradition and Reform: An Analysis of Gandhi's Political Discourse.* Rev. ed. New Delhi: Sage Publications, 1999.

Pinney, C. *Camera Indica: The Social Life of Indian Photographs.* London: Reaktion Press, 1997.

Potter, D. *India's Political Administrators, 1919–1983.* Oxford: Clarendon Press, 1986.

Ramusack, B. *The Indian Princes and Their States.* Cambridge: Cambridge University Press, 2004.

Raychaudhuri, T. *Perceptions, Emotions, Sensibilities: Essays on India's Colonial and Postcolonial Experiences.* New Delhi: Oxford University Press, 1999.

Said, E. *Orientalism.* New York: Pantheon Books, 1978.

Seal, A. *The Emergence of Indian Nationalism: Competition and Collaboration in the Later Nineteenth Century.* Cambridge: Cambridge University Press, 1968.

Sen, A. "More Than 100 Million Women Are Missing." *The New York Review,* 10 December 1990.

Som, R. "Jawaharlal Nehru and the Hindu Code: A Victory of Symbol over Substance?" *Modern Asian Studies* 28:1(1994): 165–94.

Spangenburg, B. "The Problem of Recruitment for the Indian Civil Service in the Later Nineteenth Century." *Journal of Asian Studies* 30 (1971): 341–60.

Srivastava, S. *Constructing Post-Colonial India: National Character and the Doon School.* London: Routledge, 1998.

Symonds, R. *Oxford and Empire: The Last Lost Cause?* Oxford: Clarendon Press, 1991.

Thompson, P. *The Voice of the Past: Oral History.* 3rd ed. 1978. Oxford: Oxford University Press, 2000.

Tomlinson, B. R. *The Indian National Congress and the Raj, 1929–1942: The Penultimate Phase.* London: Macmillan, 1976.

Weiner, M. *Party Building in a New Nation: The Indian National Congress.* Chicago: University of Chicago Press, 1967.

Index

Judith M. Brown

is Beit Professor of Commonwealth History
and Professorial Fellow of Balliol College,
the University of Oxford.
She is the author of a number of books, including
Nehru: A Political Life and *Gandhi: Prisoner of Hope*.